GUENTER F. GROSS

Win at Work
and at Home!

**verlag
moderne industrie**

Published in association with the Institute of Directors

DIRECTOR BOOKS

First published in German
as *Beruflich Profi, privat Amateur? Berufliche
Spitzenleistungen und persönliche
Lebensqualität*, 5. Auflage
by verlag moderne industrie, Landsberg

English language edition published by Director Books,
an imprint of Fitzwilliam Publishing Limited,
Simon & Schuster International Group,
Fitzwilliam House, 32 Trumpington Street,
Cambridge CB2 1QY, England

First published 1991

© English language edition, Fitzwilliam Publishing Limited, 1991

British Library Cataloguing in Publication Data
Gross, Guenter F.
  Win at work and at home!
  I. Title   II. [Beruflich Profi, privat Amateur?]
  English
  303
  ISBN 1-870555-50-3

Library of Congress Cataloguing in Publication Data
Gross, Guenter F.
  [Beruflich Profi, privat Amateur? English]
  Win at work and at home!/Guenter F. Gross.
    p. cm.
  "Published in association with the Institute of Directors."
  Translation of: Beruflich Profi, privat Amateur?
  Includes index.
  ISBN 0-13-960436-7 (Prentice Hall): $19.95
  1. Work and family. 2. Quality of life. 3. Executives – Family
    relationships. I. Institute of Directors. II. Title.
  HD4904.25.G76 1991
  658.4'094–dc20   91-26117
                          CIP

Distributed in the United States by Prentice Hall
ISBN: 0-13-960436-7

Designed by Geoff Green
Typeset by Rowland Phototypesetting Limited, Bury St Edmunds, Suffolk
Printed in Great Britain by BPCC Wheatons Limited, Exeter

Contents

Preface

Do you have to live a narrow-gauge life? Is that simply the fate of the career-minded? Is a widening gap to yourself, your partner and your private life the price that simply has to be paid for winning at work?

Perhaps this one-sided fixation on your job is doing more harm than good? A ship with all its cargo stowed on one side would have capsized long ago. Does your work have to consume all of your time, energy and attention? Wouldn't you be able to enjoy much more success at work if you could strike a more harmonious balance between your work life and your private life?

Do you really have to live your life the way you do in order to be assured of professional success and security? Wouldn't it be possible to give your private life a bit more of the attention that you have been so one-sidedly devoting to your work life?

You pay so much attention to intensifying and securing your contacts with others. Isn't it time to intensify your contact with yourself, with your partner and with your children?

The world we live in today does not make it easy to live a broader-based lifestyle. We live in a world that is devoid of peace and tranquillity. There is no longer any continuity to it. It is a world that is dominated by hustle and bustle. It is a world in which certain types of personalities are becoming very rare. There are fewer and fewer lions in today's society, while the number of wolves, weasels and rabbits is on the rise.

The title of William Manchester's biography of Winston Spencer Churchill puts it quite succinctly: *The Last Lion.*

Churchill is one of the last great examples of the fact that it is possible to combine a hard-working, colourful life with a happy marriage: 'I married Clementine Hozier – and lived happily ever afterwards.'

In our work lives, our senses are honed to discovering

opportunities. Yet many of us do not even recognise that our private lives offer 'opportunities' as well. Those who are especially career-minded tend to relegate their private lives to a second-class status. How much more they could achieve for themselves and for their careers if they would only pay more attention to their private lives.

This book represents an attempt to provide a strategic concept for enhancing your personal quality of life and an overview of the actions and attitudes that will enable you to do it.

It answers the following questions: What are the rules of success for a happy marriage? What kind of attitude offers the most benefits to both husband and wife?

How can you cut down on your worries and gain an attitude that is characterised by cheerfulness and peace of mind? How can you better manage problems and stress? What active steps can you take to conserve your mental energy and vitality?

Munich, 25 May 1989   Guenter F. Gross

CHAPTER 1

Prospects for a happy relationship/marriage

Is it possible at all for a business executive with an especially successful career to lead an active, happy private life? Is it possible to combine top-at-work achievement with personal and family quality of life, or does one preclude the other? Is it perhaps possible that only someone with a mediocre career can have the time, energy and interest to devote to private life?

Do you as someone with an especially successful career want anything aside from your work life? Is that all you require to be content? Do you possess the resolve to win at home *and* at work? Might not the ideal situation for you be a pacified home front without any demands and excitement, so that you can concentrate entirely on your work interests?

Are there work dictates that make it impossible for you to devote time, energy and peace of mind to your private life, no matter how much you might wish to do so?

Why do you concentrate so one-sidedly on your work? Who and what are forcing you to do so? What are the unavoidable dictates to which you are subjected, even though they exist only in your mind? Which pressures do others pile on you, which ones do you pile on yourself? Will these pressures increase in the future? What kind of additional pressures will there be?

Until you have answered these questions for yourself, it will be impossible for you to stipulate a strategy for shaping a more fulfilled private life.

Although this book tends to speak of men with especially successful and stressful careers, it is obvious that it is equally valid for women who have especially successful careers.

The characteristics of the winners

The key to winning at work is professionalism. People are not successful because they are talented, innovative and able to shape outstanding concepts. As important as these factors may be, they are frequently overestimated in the success matrix. No organisation needs a great new concept every week. On the contrary, an organisation faced with a great new concept every week would not survive very long.

Someone who is successful and professional does not serve up one idea after another. Nor is superior intelligence the key factor. It is the ability to concentrate on implementation that brings success. Success comes because the executive devotes more time and energy than others to the implementation side of the equation.

As a winner at work you have a pronounced perception of urgency and for boldly following up on budding opportunities. You take great pains in handling routine matters, which means that you are especially alert and thus constantly interacting with numerous factors. As a result, your mind is rarely dormant; you are always thinking about one subject or another. As the saying goes: 'You can't tune out!'

Team captain and goalkeeper

As a business executive you are usually both the captain of the team and the goalkeeper. This means that you have to do double duty: you are both responsible for the team and the court of last resort.

The team's success hinges upon your stamina. You can't leave your position during the game. That would be fatal. In this situation, nothing in your private life could ever induce you to leave the playing field. Just imagine the goalkeeper's wife standing off to the side and trying to entice him off the playing field by saying: 'Just what is your job? All you're doing is standing around the whole time. That's the kind of work I'd like to have. Now I finally see what you call hard work. You call that work? Is that really something for grown men to be doing? Do you really enjoy it?

'I thought you were the captain of the team. You're always spouting off about delegating. Well why don't you finally delegate? What are all your people doing anyway? Get tough with them. Send them forward. Why are they always milling around you? If they'd run a little harder, the ball would never even get to your half of the field.

'Do you really have to be there in person? Couldn't you install an answering machine in the goal? I'll even give you the message to put on it: "Sorry, the goalkeeper is unavailable right now due to important family matters. Please call again tomorrow with the ball!"'

Back to the dictates: during the game, the goalkeeper can't allow himself to be distracted by personal factors. The game demands his undivided attention. While the opposing team is doing everything it can to fire the ball into the goal, the goalkeeper can't simply turn around and begin chatting with his wife about their plans for the evening.

This is the situation in which 'top achievers' find themselves at work. This is the situation as long as the game is being played. Conditions are different between games. What's more, those who sign up to play every game on the schedule are in an entirely different position from those who give careful thought to which games they want to play, which projects they want to do.

People who grasp at every opportunity that presents itself at work, regardless of how important or unimportant it may be, will be so busy trying greedily to grasp at them that they will bungle the quality of their private life.

The price of success today

The price that must be paid for success goes up from year to year. There are two factors that are primarily responsible for this: first of all, there is the quickening pace of change, and thus the lack of continuity and the increasingly shortened life cycle for a given set of conditions; the second factor is the competition's increasing potential for research and development, and thus change.

The ranks of the competitors are growing. Their resourcefulness is increasing. Foreign competitors are getting into high gear and are forcing you to devote more time and energy just to maintain your previous level of success.

On the other hand, you will be striking out aggressively in new directions to achieve greater success there. In this sense, the single European market will increase your potential for winning at work. In terms of your private life, though, this development is more likely to mean additional stress than to provide any relief. It is necessary to be aware of this and to take it into consideration early on.

It is this quickening pace of change that leaves you with so little energy for your private life. *Being successful* is one side of the coin, *staying successful* the other. In the past, the situation was totally different.

The more leisurely pace of change of past decades enabled you to enjoy the fruits of your success longer.

You had an idea; you implemented the idea; and then you might have been able to harvest the idea for years. Today, you sow an idea, and then you have only one season in which to harvest it. Everything you invest today in terms of new ideas provides only a brief yield of success. Then the competition catches up with you, and you can start all over again.

Today, it is only possible to pacify a business sector on a short-term basis. You are constantly being forced to stake out new claims. But hardly have you staked your claim when Genghis Khan appears on the scene and sweeps into your territory with his hordes.

This analysis would not appear to leave much hope for a happier private life and more personal quality of life. Or are there perhaps strategic approaches that would allow you to keep winning at work and still win at home? In fact, there are. But first, let's take a closer look at the situation of the professional elite.

The professional elite

Elite, in this context, is meant in terms of achievement, and thus quality. In this sense, membership of the elite is the result of perseverance and effort, as well as a pronounced sense of responsibility and achievement.

The elite live in a special type of poverty. The reason this is not recognised at first glance is that poverty is normally defined much too narrowly. Poverty is almost always viewed only in terms of the financial aspect. This narrow viewpoint results in an almost total fixation on only one factor of poverty, the financial aspect. Yet it would be naive to assess someone's wealth merely on the basis of their financial situation.

If you take a broader view of things, you will clearly recognise that the elite live in poverty. They are poor in terms of time, reflection and tranquillity. From a time standpoint, the elite actually live below the

Elite

= Talent
= Effort
= Achievement
Quality

The elite live in poverty

No time
No reflection
No tranquillity
No recognition
No sympathy
No social interaction

poverty level. The best that they can do for their personal lives is to scrape together time left-overs. It is impossible for them to carve out the best slice of time. The elite always have time debts. The account balance between what they want to accomplish and what they are actually able to accomplish is almost always in the red.

The elite run the risk of not being able to partake in important parts of what makes a successful life. If you have a successful career but are not able to forge a happy private life, you are not really living.

Managing your personal resources

Start by examining your personal resources. Look at all of your resources that could impact your energy for implementing things, and thus your ability to implement things. The faster and more energetically you overcome obstacles, the faster you will achieve your success goals. These could include either offensive or defensive measures.

The faster you handle your work tasks, the more time you have left for your marriage. And this brings us to one of your most important resources: your time. What you need is a better time strategy. In other words, what you need is a better time budget, a better time-allocation structure.

Selecting your fields of activity is absolutely crucial. You have to view every time investment just as critically as a financial investment. You normally deal with numerous projects. It is possible that 20 per cent of these projects will generate 80 per cent of your success. Of course, it is not always possible to know this in advance. Nevertheless, it is fair to say that, for a variety of reasons, most of us carelessly and unthinkingly commit ourselves to projects that offer only a marginal contribution towards our success, but which endanger the success of our other projects and force us to divert time away from our private lives.

Truly entrepreneurial personalities are also good at concentrating. They are not just resolute doers, they are even more resolute not-doers. They don't need to have a piece of all of the action, they *themselves* decide whether or not they want to be involved.

Let your marriage partner play a greater role in helping you decide how to invest and allocate your time resources.

By now, your partner is familiar with your principles. She or he knows which long-term goals you are steering for, and knows better than you which risks of distraction exist and when you are in danger of moving away from your goal. *Your partner is more objective.*

Ask your partner to pose questions to you. Statements and comments are not enough. It might take only a few questions to get you out of the clouds and back down to earth, i.e. to an objective assessment of the meaningfulness of it all. Here are several questions that you could be asked:

1. Is it a large project? How large?
2. Does it fit in with your underlying, long-term objectives? Will it bring you closer to them?
3. Are there any other projects which would then have to be neglected, which would be more difficult to implement or which would provide less benefit?
4. Do you *have* to tackle this project?
5. Is there another project that might perhaps be more meaningful and profitable?
6. What will be the benefit to you personally?
7. What advantages will it offer for our private life?
8. Is it really an extremely worthwhile project?
9. Who else besides you would benefit from it?
10. Would you tackle this project if you were only able to work six hours a day?

These were some brief comments on the subject of how to handle the resource of 'time' in a strategic manner.

Let's now take a look at the other resources, in addition to time, which are of crucial significance for your private life:

Mental energy.
Frame of mind.
Physical strength – health and fitness.

The following two chapters of this book focus on methods for keeping you in the right frame of mind and making it even better. This one deals with your 'mental energy'. Often enough, it is not the limited amount of time you have that prevents you from enjoying a happy and satisfying private life. It is your lack of mental energy. The day is over, it's evening now, and your energy has gone.

Most of us feel that it is entirely natural that our work consumes our energy and that our leisure time must then be employed to recharge our batteries.

This is a dangerous approach. We think it is a logical consequence that highly intensive work means a loss of energy and strength: 'I worked twelve hours today. I must be dog tired. You can't be fresh after working so long. Somehow, I don't feel tired, but I guess I'm wrong. I *must* be run down. That's the way it is!'

This is negative autosuggestion. Your situation at home will change dramatically if you tackle your work life from exactly the opposite standpoint. The approach is: 'My work is my hobby. I love my work. I'll arrange my work so that I can still view it as my hobby.

'I'll change my attitude in meetings, on the telephone, while writing memos and attending conferences to let in tranquillity and peace of mind. From now on, I'll resolve to work without being hurried and flustered. Being flustered, by its very nature, means taking side-steps. The more work I have to do, the slower I'll get ahead when I'm flustered.

'My goal is to gain energy as a result of my work, not to expend it. My top priority is to come home relaxed, cheerful and at ease at the end of the day. When my partner asks how I feel, I'd like to answer: "Terrific, fit as a fiddle!"'

Why not? All of the factors that prevent you from coming home this way are useless elements. They include such factors as agitation, nervousness, aggravation and worries. None of these factors helps you get ahead. They are absolutely useless. Throw them out of your office window. They're parasites. The less you have to do with these characters, the stronger and more relaxed you'll feel at home. The following chapters show you how to purge these factors from your life. But now it's time to take a closer look at the institution of marriage.

Quality of life

The quality of life is the *quality of living together*, i.e. the quality of partnerships. And the partnership that has the greatest influence on your personal happiness is your marriage.

Your marriage is your only life-long contract. It is the greatest task you'll ever face in life. It is *the* challenge to your creativity, your abilities and your imagination.

Winning in life

Your frame of mind

'What you think!'

Winning in life

Courage

Inner tranquillity

Cheerful peace of mind

No pressure

Quality of life

Quality of living together

=

The quality of your partnerships

Winning in life is what you feel and think

Winning in life means having a winning frame of mind. It relates to the quality of the thoughts in your mind.

You win in life when your anxiety remains within limits, when you have inner tranquillity, cheerfulness and peace of mind, and when you do not have the feeling that you are constantly under pressure.

Your success in achieving this objective hinges upon the quality of your work and personal partnerships. The cardinal partnership in determining how successful you will be in winning in life is your marriage.

Winning at work doesn't have to mean you're winning in life

To some it would appear to be sufficient. They are satisfied if they don't have to fight on a second front at home. They are satisfied if they succeed in more or less pacifying a second front should it occur.

For them, it is enough not to have to fight a guerrilla war at home. Long ago, they gave up all hope of being able to turn the people who share their territory into heartfelt allies.

At best, they recognise that their chances for achievement and success at work naturally depend upon the quality of their private life. They realise that problems at work are often the result of problems at home. *That's why* they do not want any problems at home.

The way they see it, everything around them is always measured only against the benchmark of its significance for their work. They do not realise that marriage is an institution *sui generis* and not merely a means to an end at work. For them, a good marriage is not a 'better marriage', but merely less of an impediment to their work life.

Front line and rear echelon

It is wrong to view your work as the front line and your private life as the rear echelon. This view relegates your private life to a mere support function. It prevents you from seeing that your private life is also a sector in which active, positive action is required.

Compared with your work, you give far too little thought to your private sector, especially your marriage, in terms of ideas and energy. There is much less strategy and professionalism in your private life. This kind of thinking and attitude is amateurish. It treats marriage not as an independent enterprise, but as a branch office, an annex, a subsidiary.

Objective in life: successful survival!

How you shape your life is also how you shape your survival. At work you know which factor it is that enables you to survive within an organisation. At work, especially in the business world, what counts is *'economic' survival*. The factor that brings this about is *financial gain*.

In marriage, survival is also what counts. Survival of the marriage and its central meaning. At work you're dealing with material survival. In marriage it's *emotional survival*. The key factor here is *tenderness*!

If tenderness is not fostered and nurtured, a marriage is a non-entity. It is an inanimate object, devoid of life.

How far ahead would we be if we were to devote just a fraction of the thought that we dedicate to the 'financial gain' factor in conjunction with our desire for success at work to this factor that is so crucial in a marriage?

Your partner at home is your most important customer

No client is as important to you as your partner, who's not just the only customer with whom you have a life-long contract, but also the only customer who is there at night. Your partner is closer to you than anyone else.

Your marriage is not an institution, it's a project

Your marriage is not something that is cut in stone and never changes. Your marriage is not static. It is not something that you once established and then said: 'That's that.'

It is the task of both husband and wife to shape their marriage. A marriage should be developed using the same approach that is so obvious in the case of a business. Your marriage, too, needs goals,

Marriage is an

Independent
enterprise

not a

Branch office

Survival

At work

Financial gain

↓

Economic survival

At home

Tenderness

↓

Emotional

survival

Your partner

The only person with whom you have
a life-long contract

Your most important customer

Your only customer who's there at night
too and to whom you supply
- Attentiveness and
- Affection

Marriage

The only life-long contract

Some prefer to lease

plans of action, perhaps even progress reports. Your marriage needs resource allocation, especially a reasonable time appropriation in your time budget.

In your work life, being and working together with other people manifests itself in a never-ending chain of meetings and conferences, at which information is provided, decisions are made, goals are set, action is planned, results are assessed.

Not much happens in this regard in your private life. In many marriages, there are never any 'conferences' on these kinds of topics. *Marriage is the only enterprise where there are no conferences.*

People who are so professional at work are blind at home, seeing neither what is nor what should be. They overlook the fact that marriage, too, requires a systematic assessment of the situation, requires creativity, goals, plans of action, success-reporting procedures and a set of rules for cooperation.

And yet, it would all be so easy for the professional at work, who possesses an entire tool kit for shaping cooperative ventures and managing projects. All that's necessary is to utilise some of those professional management tools at home.

Methods and terminology transfer

As a professional at work, all you have to do is think about the terminology you are constantly surrounded with in your work. Make a game of transferring this terminology to your private life. Then you'll recognise an entire catalogue of tasks and opportunities.

The terminology of leadership techniques clearly demonstrates this. Leadership means: 'Getting people moving and keeping them moving towards an objective.'

To accomplish this, you have to provide certain functions. They are the same functions that are encountered in a creative and dynamic private life. In your private life, too, it is necessary to address activities and achievements; to motive and encourage; to monitor and assess the results.

In your private life, too, you are faced with the tasks of communication and cooperation. It's impossible without discussions and 'conferences'.

Risk factors, problems, opportunities, goals and action cannot always be handled in passing, whenever the subject happens to arise. There are enough important topics in your private life that deserve to

Marriage is
not an institution
it's
a project!

So:

Situation analysis

Creativity

Goals

Plans of action

Progress reports

Family conference

Our

Situation

Problems

Risk factors

Opportunities

Our

Long-term goals

Goals for this year

Time budget:

Financial budget:

Joint action:

Rules for dealing with one another:

be tackled methodically, that deserve your concentration. The conclusion is: Perhaps you should hold a 'family conference' from time to time.

Prevention in your private life

The concept of prevention numbers among the greatest strategic achievements. It is a form of action and keeps you from being forced to react. In marriage, too, prevention is one of the most important strategic tasks. The later you act, the more pressure you are going to be under. In the private sphere, it is sometimes later than you think, even for world champions in self-deception. You still think that, on the whole, everything is perfectly alright. You don't notice that your partner's disillusionment has long since turned into paralysis, and that this is the only reason why things are peaceful.

A wedding ceremony is the sale, and thus the conveyance, of promises. Marriage is the realisation of these promises. It's a form of customer service. In a happy marriage, the advertising campaign begins *after* the wedding ceremony.

It is extremely difficult to lead a successful marriage unless both husband and wife have similar basic convictions, objectives and strategic concepts.

Marriage is more than just an organisational frame for a division of labour. It is first and foremost a risk-sharing joint venture, a security alliance, a mutual enjoyment partnership. The foundation of a good marriage is the pleasure of knowing that your partner exists and is the way she or he is.

Winning at work – winning at home?

Many professionals at work assume that the impressive success they enjoy at work will automatically buy success at home. This is not necessarily the case: there are enough case histories on the subject of 'Wealthy at work, impoverished at home!'

Success at work, which manifests itself in such attributes as position, influence, recognition and income, is a coin of the realm that is not necessarily accepted as legal tender in a marriage.

Undoubtedly, the attributes of your success at work are something that will also impress the partner in your private life, who, naturally, values all of these trappings of power, the honours and the medals, and is proud of you.

Achievements at work

↓

Winning at work

Position	Affection
Influence	Income
Standing	Wealth

Recognition

Winning at home

↑

Achievements at home

'Marriage marketing'

Your partner is
your most important customer

- **Advertising plan**
- **Step-by-step plan**
'Special efforts'
- **Profit planning**
Cheerfulness
Security
Inner tranquillity

Action

Yet all of these elements are the results of interaction between you and outsiders. You have achieved all of this through your contacts and ties with people who are not members of your family. Here, something is being valued whose origins stem from another playing field. What this amounts to is long-distance success.

But close-up success is important in a marriage. And this can be achieved only through acts that are performed in the private sphere. Genuine success in your private life can be brought about only through achievements made in your private life for your private life.

In your partner's eyes, what you do for other people, what other important people do for you, how others see and assess you are not the decisive factors. For your partner, direct affection and attention are what count; what ultimately counts is not the lofty pedestal on which you stand, but your closeness or distance as a partner.

The prerequisites for winning at home

As someone who is successful at work you possess many of the prerequisites for winning at home. You are professional, creative, vital, self-confident, aggressive and cheerful, and also extremely charming towards your customers.

What you don't have for and in your private life are time, energy, enthusiasm and resolve. You love your work. It is a hobby. It is to work that you devote your energy.

When you arrive home, not much of your vitality is left. Home becomes a rest home. The impressive professional at work undergoes a metamorphosis as soon as you cross the threshold. You become institutionalised. Your creativity goes on holiday to recharge its batteries.

From the standpoint of someone who is under tremendous pressure at work, this is all very well and good. Why shouldn't it be? Fortunately, alertness, vitality, prudence and caution are not necessary at home. Because the only human being in the world who really wants what's best for you lives at home.

At home, you can let yourself go. Here, you don't have to choose every word with such great care. Here, you can forget the principles of aesthetics, and cast off clothing that is designed to impress others and slip into old textile friends.

Here, you can shed all of the limitations, inhibitions and caution.

Winners at work

Professional

Creative

Vital

Self-confident

Aggressive

Cheerful

Charming

In other words,

many of the

prerequisites needed

to be a winner

at home!!!

'All' that's still required:

Time	**Strength**
Interest	**Resolve**

Here is where love lives. Here, you don't need any self-discipline. Or that's what you think!

Unfortunately, there is such a thing as a marriage paradox: 'Marriage is the only partnership in which you can cast caution to the winds in complete safety. Assuming, however, that you go about it with extreme caution. Because only then will you be assured of love, affection and benevolence!'

How do you treat whom?

This is a question that is easy for you to answer. You need only study your behaviour on the telephone. Is it possible that you treat a strange caller differently from your family when they call? Could your behaviour be governed by the following rule: 'the stranger the better'?

Could it be that you are more relaxed, at ease and cordial towards customers and other business associates than towards your own family?

Are you perhaps more cautious, thoughtful, painstaking and attentive with your business associates?

Should this be the case, how absurd it would be! It can only mean that you feel the others are more important than your family.

This greater importance that you attach to others can only be explained, in turn, by the fact that the others represent more of a danger to you or will not offer you as much if you are not especially helpful and solicitous.

The only logical conclusion with respect to your partner at home would be that you feel there is no way her or his attitude towards you could be influenced by your own attitude. The foolhardiness of this kind of reasoning is obvious.

The ones who should receive your ultimate fondness and kindness are your family. They need your patience, cheerfulness and peace of mind. Those at home should be the first to partake in what you have the power to provide in terms of affection, cordiality and tact.

Your work – more exciting than your private life?

'Work is toil and drudgery!' That might be how people see it who are unsuccessful at work, because they are frustrated. For them

The marriage paradox

The only partnership in which you
can safely
- Cast caution to the winds
- Let yourself go

Assuming, however, that you go about
it with extreme care and caution at
all times
In both your words and deeds

The stranger – the better

1. Cautious
2. Thoughtful
3. Painstaking
4. Attentive
5. Imaginative
6. Cordial
7. Vital

Absurd!!!

Who's calling?

A customer:
'I always have time for you. As much
as you want!'
Cordial, relaxed, cheerful

A member of your family:
'Oh it's you again. What's happened
this time?'
Impatient, hurried, unfriendly

everything involved with work is uninteresting, boring and burdensome. For those who are successful at work, the exact opposite holds true. They are the centre of attraction in a modern circus. For them there are 'thrills and chills galore' every day. Work offers so much excitement and variety that they have no need for any further adventure at home.

If you are someone who is successful at work, your private life is in order if *as little as possible* happens. You are happily married to your work. You have no intention of playing the bigamist and leading a second marriage at home.

What you experience on the stage of work would be impossible to achieve at home without huge financial outlays and knowing all the right people. Your private life deteriorates not because of stress at work, but precisely because work is so interesting and satisfying.

If you only had more time to do all the other things you could do at work, the world would truly be in order. Fortunately, your private life offers a major advantage. Should you happen to need some additional time for work life, there are still sufficient time reserves in your private life that can be tapped.

The consequences of this kind of reasoning can remain concealed for a very long time, because the erosion at home is an extremely gradual process. Somewhere along the line, though, it does finally arrive: the moment of truth. The solution is simple: 'Wake up earlier!'

How are you at home?

In addition to time, many people who are successful at work lack the mental energy and physical strength for their private lives. Many are in a constant state of tension. Rarely are they relaxed. Their heads are filled with foreign armies of occupation. A parade of topics and issues marches through their minds, plundering them of their energy.

They arrive home worn out by stress, are not really there. Their bodies are at home, but their minds are still at the office. At home, they live the life of a zombie: 'How did you like dinner tonight?' 'Why do you ask? Have we already eaten?'

Physically, they are free to move about at will. But their thoughts are not free. Here, they are constantly preoccupied and under pressure. Every day, something unexpected happens to them. They are never alone, together only with themselves and their thoughts.

Is your husband home yet?

Yes, part of him!

His body has just arrived.

But his mind is still at the office.

I expect it will follow in half an hour.

They are constantly entwined in a mesh of dependencies. The spirit of cooperation they feel is so necessary at work forces them to be considerate of the interests of many other people.

All of this makes it so difficult for them really to be there and present in their private life.

One of the reasons for this might be that they show up at home too suddenly. This is understandable in view of the limited amount of time that they have for their private life; they want to use every remaining minute for it.

Perhaps it would be better if they took a short break before coming home. It is wrong to show up at home directly after an especially hard day at work. The 'bends' should give food for thought. This is an illness that occurs if a diver returns to the surface too quickly after 'working under pressure'.

Put yourself in quarantine for a while every time you've had a hard day at work. Give yourself time to calm down. Don't rush home. It's better to come home relaxed and at ease.

Don't show up at home in a state that makes it necessary for you first to clear your head of everything that has collected in it. You should not arrive home loaded down with the day's baggage, but free and receptive. *Come as someone whose mind is cleared of burdens.*

What role do you play at home? Is your home the stage for a solo performance starring you? Or is it the exact opposite – a training camp for a Trappist monastery?

Is it an old-clothes fashion show, featuring the wardrobe you have collected over the past few decades?

Is your work Charm Stadium and your home Complaint City?

What is your home? What does it mean to you? What role do you play in it? What do you perform there, a symphony or a string quartet? Is it a huge variety show, with you juggling twelve balls at once? Or is it an impressive temple of boredom, where you constantly roll the same ball back and forth?

Out with anxiety, in with happiness!

Once you have recognised the key goals for your marriage, it will be relatively easy for you to take the right action and develop a meaningful attitude.

But what are the goals for a good marriage? Each of us will have

The bends

=

Returning to the surface too quickly after working under pressure.

Give yourself time to calm down!
Don't rush home!

An illness unknown in cities with lots of good pubs:
Because there's a 'decompression station' at every corner.

How did you like dinner tonight?

Why do you ask? Have we already eaten?

Zombie!

The man with the automatic jaws

My home?

Solo performance

Old-clothes fashion show

Reading room

Complaint City

our own. However, the selection of truly basic goals is not very large. In ranking the goals for a good marriage, tenderness comes first.

This is followed by two other main goals: *Free your partner at home from anxiety and foster his or her happiness.*

That's easy to say. When both you and your partner have achieved these two goals, you will have brought about something absolutely fascinating and out of the ordinary. 'Free your partner from anxiety'; what do you achieve by doing this? Your partner feels secure, and does not hover in a state of uneasiness, but has the feeling of being protected. Your partner trusts in your integrity, energy and strength. The ground does not yield underfoot, but feels like a firm foundation.

'Foster his or her happiness' means more than just making sure your partner is cheerful. It means giving his or her life luxury. Happiness allows your partner to open up, not to feel encircled or chained down, not restricted. You give your partner the thrill of exuberance.

Exuberance is 'deluxe freedom'

Let's come back to the goal of 'freeing your partner at home from anxiety'. You'll recall that 'freedom from fear' is the cornerstone in the foundation for quality of life. Many do not pay enough attention to this point.

They act carelessly. Instead of giving their partner a feeling of safety and security in every possible way, they are constantly riding as couriers of impending doom.

They have a tremendous repertoire of disturbance, fear and anxiety triggers. They use their marriage as a dumping ground for entire arsenals of fear.

They pile fears upon their partner and leave him or her buried under the heap. With a sombre face, they don't give up until they have unloaded everything.

Then their expression suddenly changes. They are overcome by a feeling of happiness. Freed of their burden, they walk away whistling cheerfully, leaving behind their partner buried under a heap of negative rubble.

Motivate your partner at home

At work, so much is said about 'motivation' that we almost can't bear to hear any more. At home, on the contrary, it would appear that the

Marriage goals

- Free your partner from anxiety
- Foster your partner's happiness

The ultimate benefit:

'Peace of mind'

= At ease

= Unharmed

= Secure

Courage – the basis for quality of life

List of

Disturbance

Fear } triggers

Anxiety

Negative imagination?

Couriers of impending doom?

Partner A   Partner B

Anxiety   ⟶   Depression

Marriage is no dumping ground for arsenals of fear

task of 'motivation' does not even exist at all. There is definitely a lot of catching up to be done here. If anyone needs motivation, it is your partner.

Your partner's self-confidence must be fostered and strengthened. He or she should *never* be degraded, but helped to develop talents and strengths. Show your enthusiasm and pleasure about your partner's achievements and capabilities.

Be generous with your praise, recognition and admiration. Put your partner on a pedestal.

Make obvious the combination of joy, affection and admiration that you feel when he or she moves, says something or does something.

Don't horde the interesting, mentally challenging activities for yourself. Fight to ensure that your partner has tasks that are just as fascinating, varied and mentally challenging as your own. This will not be an easy task. You'll need ideas for it.

Partner or errand-runner?

Don't degrade your partner at home. If rules for dealing with others are important at work, they're vital at home. Don't turn your partner into a hired hand or errand-runner.

Make sure your partner has space, but isn't left alone nor constantly crowded. Attention is one side of the coin; the other side, which is just as important, is 'respectful' distance. Don't become your partner's educator. Being caring and courteous will keep him or her attractive.

Rules for treating a partner whose work is especially stressful

If your partner's working life is extremely stressful, you will not make his or her private life more fulfilled by constantly producing demands, admonishments and criticism.

The only way to win a partner who works over to a better private life is to avoid making constant demands, and to make it as easy and pleasurable as possible to slip into home life.

This partner has neither the time nor the energy to be responsible for organising every detail of your private life.

Self-confidence

- Foster it
- Strengthen it

Never be degrading

Talents and strengths
- Develop them
- Allow them to be used

No welfare terror

The art of creative praise

- Indirect

Non-verbal

- Surprising

Imagination

in demonstrating

- Affection

- Admiration

Challenging work

The way to become an achiever

I

want to become an achiever too!!!

Of course!
Go out in the garden and mow the lawn.

Confidence in your partner

'Do you think it's right

for you to simply go out and disappear

while I have all this work to do?'

'Yes, I have complete confidence in you

and I know that you'll keep working hard

even if I'm not watching you!'

So if *you* have a bit more time, you should utilise creativity and organisational talent and take charge in shaping a varied private life.

Someone whose work is especially stressful has to be able simply to slip into home life, without having to take any organisational steps or other action. If your partner says, 'Tomorrow I'll be able to devote the entire day to our private life', be happy about it. If, nevertheless, a work call becomes necessary the next morning, don't make any snide remarks. Allow your partner peace of mind with this phone call.

Of course, the exact opposite could also occur. But take the risk. Don't attempt to forbid your partner from engaging in any kind of work-related activity. Be generous and willing to compromise.

Don't say: 'This is just how I imagined "the entire day for our private life". I thought we had agreed that you would devote today to your family. And now you're on the phone again. Well, I guess that was my day. Why don't you go back to your beloved work. As far as I'm concerned, we don't have to do anything today!'

This kind of treatment is unkind. It doesn't benefit anyone. The less you put your partner under pressure, the faster he or she will regain energy. Your caring, understanding and generosity will enable him or her to do what *you* would like.

Relentless demands don't benefit anyone. Instead, support your partner in the struggle for liberation. The more assistance you provide here, the more you will be rewarded with his or her cheerful presence. The relaxation and tranquillity that you supply will be returned to you.

Talking with you about the subjects of concern will clear your partner's mind, and there will be a greater chance that you'll be able to get around to subjects that interest both of you.

Help your partner make decisions, so that he or she can put aside the subjects that are constantly nagging. Being able or not to make a decision also depends upon how you are likely to respond to the new situation that develops as a result of the decision. You can let your partner know beforehand, so that there will be less worry about the future.

Don't attempt to hurt your partner. You will be gradually eroding more and more of him or her. Give more thought to how you can keep this person intact. If you do, you will also be keeping him or her this way for yourself.

Mouse or spouse?

Make . . . !

Do . . . !

Get . . . !

Bring . . . !

Do it yourself for once!

Where are you?

What are you doing?

When are you coming?

Leave him/her 'alone' 'in peace'

Charming, cordial partner or overbearing educator?

'Just be still and listen to us for thirty minutes. That way we can profit from our conversation, and you might even learn something!'

Result: How to turn an onlooker into a sniper

Don't degrade your partner. Don't maliciously destroy the ability to achieve. Foster his or her happiness.

You *yourself* are responsible for shaping your life. It is not your partner's duty and obligation to make everything turn out the way you'd like, but success in doing so, of course, is all the better.

Your partner is certainly not the one who has to satisfy your 'legal entitlement to happiness'. You get not what you demand, but what you give. The more resolutely you yourself shape your life, based always upon the objective of a life together, the more you'll get.

What you supply in the way of ideas and preparation for things to do together will be returned to you in the form of enthusiastic participation.

Foster your partner's mental energy and frame of mind.

Use the same kind of long-term planning in your private life that your partner uses at work. In fact, it is best to plan on an even longer term at home; that way, it is more likely that you will be able to arrange for free time together. Enter your personal appointments in each other's appointment books.

Don't be disappointed if some of this free time that you've reserved is then used for work. Private life is really the only time reserve that can be tapped for sudden work needs. Being able to draw upon time from private life to cover an unexpected workload will give your partner an enormous feeling of liberation. This might mean that you would have to set out one or two days later on holiday, but then you'll be together with a different person. Free of stress. Your partner will enjoy peace of mind, be relaxed and, naturally, will seem several years younger.

Help your partner break out of the encirclement. Give him or her support in getting free of certain battle fronts. These might be certain subjects, positions and cooperative endeavours.

Time has to be invested if your partner is to be free of a battle front. It costs time and energy for forces to be regrouped.

You do not have a legal entitlement to have your partner shape your life. You need financial resources to shape your life. It is difficult enough today to obtain these financial resources alone.

Your partner needs to be supplied with energy for home life. It is the task of each partner in a marriage to give this energy to the other.

If the focal point of your own activities tends to be your private life, then it is you who are responsible for your partner's recreation, for re-charging his or her batteries.

If you both work, then each has to assume this task for the other. Each serves as a source of strength and energy for the other.

Neither of you can sit back and expect to receive without giving anything yourself. Neither can demand that the other be solely responsible for shaping your entire private life together.

Someone who is under a great deal of stress at work is constantly thinking about work. It is difficult to be free of it.

Freeing your partner of thoughts that are a burden and steering him or her towards other topics is an art. Elements of this art are interest, understanding and circumspection.

If you offer up your own topics in the form of lamentations and complaints, your topics will not be enticing.

With a spoonful of vinegar, you'll never succeed in enticing a busy bee away from its search for the nectar to be found in the meadows of work.

A spoonful of honey is an entirely different story. You have to become a specialist in various types of honey; then the busy bee will quickly arrive on the scene.

Being in the right?

Marriage is not a courtroom. Nor is it a one-room schoolhouse. Marriage is not a question of: 'Who is in the right?'

Marriage exists as a forum for demonstrating affection. It aims at protection and security for both husband and wife. Decisions and actions should be based upon what is meaningful, and not upon how a judge would rule on the question of 'right' or 'wrong'.

Putting on a victory parade, accompanied by that famous old march, 'Come admire the victor and listen to the proof. I was right!' is a combination of stupidity and comedy: 'But you have to admit that I was right. I think I've proved to you that you were wrong. Why don't you finally admit that I'm right and you're wrong? Why don't you want to admit that I'm right!'

The choice is up to you: 'To be in the right or to have fun. To win your point or to win affection!'

Trifles

Peace of mind is part and parcel of leading a successful life together. However, you will only succeed in achieving it if you develop the ability to keep from getting upset about every trifle.

Being in the right?

The choice is yours

Being in the right   or   **Having fun**

Marriage abilities

Inability

to get upset about trifles

Ability

to change an intolerable situation

quickly and effectively

Another ability is necessary, though: the resolve not to put up with intolerable situations for long, but to change them swiftly and effectively.

There's a big difference between peace of mind and paralysis.

Generosity and affection

Of course, your partner at home does not always act the way you would wish, and, of course, may not be talked out of everything that you view as being nonsensical and perhaps risky, but will do it anyway. By following your advice, everything would have turned out better. The catastrophe would not have occurred.

Now your partner is confronted with the result of some foolishness, and comes whimpering to you. And now you're going to give him or her a piece of your mind. Now you can recall your warning and how you foresaw everything that would happen.

Why do you want to explain all that? What's the benefit? Do you really have to douse your partner with cold water? Do you have to provide a checklist detailing his or her foolish behaviour?

Don't reserve your sympathy only for those instances when your partner finds him- or herself in an unpleasant situation that was not self-made.

You should also offer sympathy if your partner was responsible for getting him- or herself into this predicament. In these cases, especially, what's needed is not a cold lecture, but sympathy and support.

The language of your marriage

The language of your marriage reveals the condition of your marriage. There is a cold, sober language, and there is a tender and loving language. There is a reproachful language and a circumspect language. There is terminology for routine matters and normal events, and there is terminology for unusual situations.

Every word that you use influences your partner's mood. Your language can put your partner in a cheerful frame of mind: it can provide the strength to act or it can paralyse.

As someone with a successful career you would never have reached your present position with language that is lame and careless. At work, your language is resolute. Use the same language at

A dousing with cold water

It's your own fault

I have no sympathy with you

That was bound to happen

And I can tell you why

Warm, gentle rain

Settle down first

Make yourself comfortable first

Now let's have a Piña Colada together

New language – new marriage

**Purge the conditional tense from
your vocabulary**

'We should have'

'We should'

'We might'

We will!!!

home. Purge the conditional tense from your at-home vocabulary: 'You should have, we should have, we might, we should!'

From now on, say: 'We will!' With this type of language, you will foster everything that is important for your marriage.

Informational hygiene

Think about how cautiously and gingerly you act when you pass on information in your work life: 'Should I speak with him about it? When should I mention it to him? What would be the best way to get the point across? Perhaps it would be better to put it in writing? When should I confront him with it? Who should definitely not hear about it?'

Although you deal with information carefully at work, you might very well be treating it carelessly at home. Time and time again, the wrong approach is taken here: 'At home, it's not necessary to weigh each word!' Exactly the opposite is true.

Be especially cautious with information in your private life. Consider exactly which information you should provide and which you should not.

Don't carelessly turn your partner into an enemy of your work and the people with whom you deal.

You make life easy for yourself at home. Enthusiastically or in a rage, you tell your partner what's on your mind. You get rid of all those negative bits and pieces. She or he sits there as though being hit by a ton of bricks.

Then your partner has to crawl out from under that heap of negative bits and pieces. And before she or he has even succeeded, you're already there with a new load.

In this situation, it is virtually inconceivable that your partner will still have any pleasant feelings left for your work and your associates.

If you've destroyed your partner's positive attitude towards your work through the careless way in which you've provided information, you will no longer be able to expect support for your work activities.

Your standard topics

It would be a miracle if you didn't have any standard topics. Perhaps these topics are all you've been talking about for months. Which ones are they? What do you talk about? Whom do you talk about?

Informational hygiene

List of your standard topics

What?

About whom?

Which topics get short-changed?

Percentage of your conversations:

Positive?

Negative?

Don't always start right in with

***your* topics**

Don't carelessly turn your partner

into an enemy of

Your work

Your associates

Is there a topic or a person seated right there at the table every time you sit down to a meal together? Do you even have an opportunity to talk with your partner at home in private, or is there someone or something else that is occupying your mind and always butting in?

Which topics that are important to your partner never come up at all when you talk together? Which topics get short-changed? Which topics do you avoid? Which topics are virtually impossible for you to speak about?

Which topics are you always dishing up to make it impossible for your partner to talk about his or her topics? 'Just be sure you don't stop talking about your topics, otherwise he or she might be able to get a word in edgewise!'

Examine your sentences and take a look at the freight these sentences are transporting. What are you transporting with your sentences? Garbage or delicacies? Are you transporting positive or negative freight? What is the percentage of positive topics and what is the percentage of negative topics in your conversations?

Would you term yourself a 'one-topic person' this week, or as a general rule for that matter? Do you see an opportunity finally to get rid of that topic? There is an opportunity: 'Initiative rids you of re-run topics!' Initiative is a prime success factor. Initiative quickly banishes negativism.

My topics – your topics

Do you always start off every conversation with your own topics? Or do you first give your partner at home an opportunity to introduce one? Do you listen patiently? Are you just as disciplined as during a meeting with an important business associate? Are you sufficiently at ease? Does the way you listen give your partner the energy, drive and ability for self-expression in a relaxed and convincing manner?

The normal situation in a marriage is that both husband and wife are talking *about me, me and me*. Break the bonds of normality. Be different. Refuse to speak only about yourself and your own topics.

Prepare yourself just as intensively for conversations with your partner as you would for important business talks.

Why shouldn't your talks at home have an agenda too? Why shouldn't you stipulate a timetable here? When you want to have serious discussion about something in your private life, why not

One-topic person

**Initiative
rids you of
re-run topics**

Communication in a marriage

Normal

She   **About herself**
⟵
and her topics

He   **About himself**
⟵
and his topics

Out of the ordinary

She   **About him**
⟶
and his topics

He   **About her**
⟶
and her topics

preplan it with a written outline? What reasons are there for not doing it?

Actually, it's all so simple. In your work life, you employ superb communication skills. Why not utilise some of these methods and tools from your work in your private life?

At work, you might use an overhead projector. You show diagrams and charts. They make things less complicated; they generate enthusiasm; they're spellbinding. Why don't you use these kinds of tools at home too? Is that really so absurd?

Let's say you're planning your holiday. You want to explain something to your partner. Simply project a few pictures on the wall so that you can both look at them and plan your holiday together.

If you utilise your professional arsenal in your private life, you'll be soaring to a new plane of success at home.

Rational – emotional

'Please be rational! What you're saying and how you're saying it is totally illogical, it's purely emotional!' Who says your partner at home has to act rationally? Why act logically? Take a look at your business associates, your superiors, colleagues, staff and customers. Do they think logically? Do they act rationally? Are they free of emotion? It is simply naive to assume that the people in your work life act rationally. It is with good reason that Herbert Alexander Simon won the Nobel Prize for Economics. His achievement was to demonstrate that business decisions are by no means always made on a rational basis.

Don't go overboard in complaining to your partner about being emotional and illogical; help him or her become calm, cheerful and at ease. Only then will it be possible to see things differently and act differently.

You don't need to do anything right away if your partner says that a certain situation is unbearable one minute longer. It's enough for you to express sympathy for that emotional situation.

If your partner is acting emotionally, it would be amateurish for you to counter with rational evidence if your goal is to help in reaching a more objective assessment of the situation.

Objectivity is the last thing in the world that's useful now. At this moment, what's needed is warmth and sympathy, and not a sober enumeration of facts.

Communication in a marriage

'I can't get this nail hammered into
the wall!'
'See, I always told you we shouldn't
have moved to Birmingville'

Passing each other like ships in the night

Specifics ———→

←——— Basics

There is something barbaric about responding to your partner's emotionality with a sober enumeration of facts; it is grotesque enough for a clown's act in a circus.

Specifics – generalities?

Your partner at home is upset about a certain situation, or is bothered by a specific factor, or is not getting ahead with a task. Instead of coming to grips with this one factor, you issue a major policy statement.

It is pointless to conduct a conversation in which your partner is always receiving *generalities* in response to *specifics*.

How good is your memory?

Be easy to be with. Don't get on your partner's nerves. As we grow older, our long-term memory tends to improve, while our short-term memory deteriorates. We can remember every old story, but not what we just said two minutes ago.

It happens time and time again: 'Here comes the cue – here comes the story!' Right on cue, your vocal cords become dissociated from your brain and start operating on their own. All your new friends love the story, but your partner just stands there looking devastated and can't bear to hear the old saw any more.

Having heard this story more than a hundred times, your partner is overcome by terror and depression the moment the cue is uttered.

Your own reaction is just the opposite. When the cue is voiced, your facial expression changes, inner vitality and radiance surge through you. There's no stopping you now: 'Did I ever tell you the story about . . . ?' 'Yes, just the other day!'

So the next time you hear the cue and feel the urge to tell the story: don't do it.

We all know that it's useless to resist the urge to tell a story. But try anyway!

What can't your partner at home bear to hear any more?

Most marriage partners are generous. Time and time again, they listen to the same old tirades with the patience of a saint. In the

'I can't bear it one minute more!'

'Good, I'll do something about it immediately.'
'Why the rush?
What's the hurry?
Can't we finally talk about it calmly?'
'But we have to do something about it!'
'Why do you always want to change everything?'

future, make a game of putting colour, variety and surprise into your conversations. Keep your audience on the edge of their seats.

Draw up a list of taboos. Note which words, formulations and standard sentences you are going to purge from your vocabulary. Turn yourself into a new person for your partner in your conversations too.

What can't your partner at home bear to see any more?

What gets on your partner's nerves? Which objects cause complaint? Which clothes arouse anger? Your partner says: 'I can't stand that old jacket any more!' And you sing a love song about your favourite blazer.

Celebrities would never dream of surrounding themselves with trappings that their fans can't stand. Why are you struggling to hang on to objects in your private life that degrade you in your partner's eyes, instead of upgrading you?

Instead of stubbornly and insensitively struggling to keep what your partner doesn't like, perform a dramatic act of liberation. Your partner says: 'I don't like that suit on you. I've never liked that 1930s suit!'

You say: 'Thanks for telling me that. I refuse to allow this outfit to insult your eyes one moment longer!'

Then pick up a pair of scissors and begin cutting up the suit into little pieces. The strategic rule is: 'Using a dramatic effect while performing a destructive act to gain affection.' You can use the same method on furniture that's out of favour. Though of course, you'll need different tools.

Aesthetics

Your marriage partner enjoys an inalienable right to expect good looks and good grooming from you. As we grow older, it is natural to spend more time on grooming, not less.

We can't stay the way we are. We can't let chance dictate what we become. Elements of the way you look and act that aggravate your partner and have thus far merely amused the perpetrator belong on a list of taboos as well.

In the broad sense, aesthetics includes not only our appearance,

Be easy to be with

- **Always new!**
- **Never entirely predictable!**

Long-term memory

Age

Short-term memory

+ Phenomenal memory when it comes to old stories

·/. Total lack of memory – 'When was the last time I told it?'

A certain cue ⟹ A certain story

Be easy to be with

What can't your partner bear to
hear any more?

Which
Words?
Formulations?
Questions?
Remarks?
Stories?

Be easy to be with

**What can't your partner bear to
see any more?**

Which

Objects?

Clothes?

TV programmes?

'I've had this hat on my head longer than
I've had you around.'
'That hat's not going!'

but also the way we act and behave. Stop doing everything that irritates your partner and affects his or her frame of mind. Stubbornly refusing to change bad habits won't make your life any better. Some people don't use a pen to write, they use it to make noise with; others think they were given fingers so they can drum on tables with them.

A successful executive related with amazement that his wife had said to him: 'Please don't eat like a . . . !' His totally insensitive response: 'Why not, we're at home!'

Second-hand life

What follows will undoubtedly be less applicable if both husband and wife have interesting jobs. If one of you has an interesting job, but your partner has more to do with the household than with other people, there are several things that will be necessary for the partner with the interesting job to do.

To a business person whose job offers a great deal of variety, peace and uniformity at home might be paradise. It offers rest and relaxation after the hard day's grind.

To the partner at home, it can be an atmosphere of dull routine which lacks contact with interesting people and demanding challenges. The partner in business is bombarded with contacts. All the partner at home ever gets are stories about contacts. This partner leads a second-hand life and feels increasingly alone, and so becomes isolated and depressed.

Provide the remedy. There's no chance of things going well if monotony is allowed to remain.

You need gentle hills in the flatlands of the routine. You need to make and cultivate friendships, you need to get together with interesting people. By no means will it be enough for you to achieve this only for yourself. You'll be destroying your partner at home if you allow this isolation to continue!

The Neptune marriage

Many of us lead a Neptune marriage. We who work surface briefly, stab with our trident and then disappear again into the depths of our sea of work. Our interludes on the surface are too short for us to catch our breath and establish ourselves on land.

We are constantly swimming from fish to fish in the ocean of our

Second-hand life

Hardly any contact with interesting

people.

Lack of demanding challenges.

Alone

Isolated

Insecure

Contacts   Stories about contacts

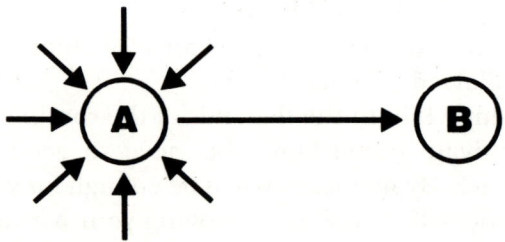

The Neptune marriage

**Surface briefly, stab with your trident
and then disappear into the depths
again.**

**Interludes on the surface too short to
catch breath.**
Constantly swimming from fish to fish.

work. Like whales, we surface briefly, blow a huge spout, and then disappear again into the sea.

What are the risk factors that threaten a marriage?

In your work life, any other project that involved the significance and magnitude of your marriage would be subjected to an intensive scrutiny of its risk factors. So, what are the risk factors that threaten a marriage?

They include the inability to understand what might perhaps be an entirely different set of values; or to comprehend the thinking patterns and feelings of your partner at home.

Another risk factor is the inability to read signs, and having the mentality of a steamroller as it insensitively rumbles right over these signs. Or yet the inability to recognise how certain behaviour patterns of your own have become intolerable to your partner over the course of time and are having a fatal effect on your relationship.

Routine is a further factor. Routine spreads a dull film of dust on a marriage. It takes away all the special spark and enthusiasm that once was there. Routine is the cause of paralysis. Everything just keeps on going the same old way; nothing out of the ordinary ever happens any more. There is nothing to look forward to with eager excitement.

Subjugation. All that remains for the partner at home is a life that is run exclusively by the partner who is in business, who becomes the measure of all things. The latter is the decision maker; the former merely a camp follower. It is no longer a partnership, just a relationship between the dominator and the dominated.

Being *over-demanding* robs the partner at home of confidence; being *under-demanding* robs him or her of energy and perhaps even of health.

Your *self-aggrandisement* forces your partner into a darkened corner. He or she stands in the shadows; you yourself stand in the limelight.

Fear reduces dignity; it degrades. Fear destroys life. It is the most horrible of all.

The *desire to dominate* and your knee-jerk urge to be the centre of attraction, something you no longer even consciously perceive, degrade your partner, who is only using 10 per cent of his or her mental abilities in the role of support player.

Risk factors in marriages

Inability to understand your partner's

- **Values**
- **Thinking patterns**
- **Feelings**

Inability to read signs

Inability to recognise principles and behaviour patterns that have become intolerable

Routine – each day exactly like the next!

Risk factors in marriages

Subjugation

- Relinquishing your own personality
- Living life only through your partner

Asking too little of your partner

Asking too much of your partner

Domination

Self-aggrandisement

Fear

Risk factors in marriages

Hectic atmosphere

Monologues

Degrading lectures and remarks

Nagging

Quarrelling over insignificant topics

Lack of aesthetics

An atmosphere that is *hectic* forces all peace of mind out of your private life. *Monologues* browbeat your partner. Degrading lectures and remarks rob him or her of dignity and inflict permanent injury.

Nagging and quarrelling over insignificant topics destroy youth and make everyone involved in this game seem very old.

Aesthetic failings degrade the one who is guilty of this breach and are an insult to the other.

What won't help?

Merely having the good will to lead a happy private life won't help. Brief, one-shot supreme efforts and good starts won't help either. You should put an end to the same old, unsuccessful efforts. You need new methods.

Bestowing financial gifts will cheer up your partner for a while, but this is no substitute for bestowing personal affection. Its effect decreases from year to year. The amount that bought you two days of cheerfulness five years ago might only be good for cheerfulness from 8:00 to 10:00 a.m. today.

Nor is an increase in material possessions necessarily a success factor. Material possessions require care and cost money to maintain. Perhaps it is precisely these additional material possessions that are forcing you to work even more so that you wind up with even less time for your private life. When this happens, material possessions become dictators. As Ralph Waldo Emerson expressed it in the last century: 'My cow milks me!'

Nor can references to the enormous financial security that your partner at home will one day enjoy be very impressive at the present time. Future security has nothing to do with the present moment; it is a promise for the future. A typical conversation demonstrates this quite clearly. The partner who's in business says: 'When I'm pushing up daisies one day, you'll be financially secure!' The partner at home responds: 'But you won't go!'

A litany of your own achievements is boring to the listener. Sooner or later, constant recitations of your own worries, problems and fears will get on the listener's nerves.

Naturally, a marriage is a partnership in which mutual worries and problems should be able to be discussed; but not all the time and without any discipline whatever.

It's intolerable to rattle off wildly one worry after another and then

What won't help

Good will

One-off supreme efforts

The same old, unsuccessful efforts

Financial bribery

Possessions

Enormous financial security

**Satisfying your partner's every
material wish**

What won't help

Litany of your own achievements

Recitations of your own worries,

problems and fears

Pleading for understanding

Shouting

Threatening

Fleeing into illness

say two days later: 'No, that's no problem at all. Of course it will be alright!'

Shouts and threats are the worst. The weak use them as an imitation of strength.

Fleeing into illness could be more dangerous than seeing a difficult situation through.

It's safer to nurse your home life.

Promises

A marriage consists of various phases that each offer different possibilities. During the initial years of marriage, you can still promise a great deal with a high degree of credibility.

When you say: 'Everything will be different in the future, I just need to accomplish . . .', your 25-year-old partner at home will still believe your every word.

Ten years later, your marriage finds itself in an entirely different phase. Your credibility has declined. You'll no longer be able to convince your partner with the same promises. At this point, actions really do speak louder than words.

What helps?

Begin by identifying what makes your partner's existence so special to you, and always view it as being something that is extraordinary, never something that is normal.

See your partner's special, positive traits. Recognise how much is offered; don't just look at what is lacking.

Try to remember and identify what and how your partner at home once used to be. Think about what you could do gingerly to restore what has been injured or lost.

Assertiveness and taker qualities might number among your basic repertoire of skills at work. What you need at home are understanding and giver qualities.

Tenderness ranks above all else. It can't be produced by activities, it is the result of a character trait.

At first glance, it might seem as if tenderness were the strength of the weak. Usually, the exact opposite holds true. The strong are the ones who can give tenderness and who have the strength to protect those who are special to them.

Famous last words:

'Everything will be different in the future'

'I just need to accomplish . . .'

Wife (25):

Still believes everything

Ayesha Hopeful

Wife (35):

No longer believes anything

Angela Scepticism

Wife (45):

Believes somewhere else

Betty Bye-Bye

- **Assertiveness**
- **Taker qualities**

- **Understanding**
- **Giver qualities**

Tenderness
- **Not an activity, it's a character trait**
- **Not weakness**

Weakness $\longrightarrow$ Terror

Strength $\longrightarrow$ Generosity

You don't need to have a face of stone to act aggressively

Do more to keep your strength from being sapped by your work life. Shape your work so that you can better conserve your mental energy and your cheerful peace of mind.

Break the bonds of routine. Research and development programmes are necessary at home too.

Establish a system for gathering a readily available database of ideas for anti-routine campaigns at home.

Put more surprise into your private life. A surprise offers more than just a change of pace. It is indicative of a very great deal. Your partner will view your surprise as a sign of how much you are thinking about him or her, as an indication that you want to please, and that you have expended time and effort to give this surprise.

Unknown to your partner, you have spent a long time making preparations to do something special. *A surprise is the tip of the iceberg. That's why surprise parties are so enjoyable.*

In your time budget, allocate time for private-life activities together with your partner. Make 'anti-appointments' in your calendar. When you make an appointment, you are giving others a claim to your time. Anti-appointments, on the contrary, are appointments that you reserve for yourselves. They are the stuff of which hope springs eternal.

Don't assume that it is your partner at home who bears the primary responsibility for getting your marriage off to a fresh start. You can't change your partner with demands. You can't influence him or her by appeals to change. You will be totally unsuccessful if you say 'I'm really curious to see all the new changes in our marriage!'

The only person you can change is yourself. This is your only possibility for turning your partner into a different person and a different partner. But it is you who are at the starting line. Good luck!

Routine can bore you to death

- Idea database for anti-routine

  campaigns at home

  - Surprises
  - Gratitude
  - Gift marketing

More planning for campaigns at home

- Be new
- Be surprising

'Amazement' programme

- **More alertness**
- **More interest**
- **More sensitivity**
- **More creativity**
- **More energy**
- **More time**
- **More speed**
- **More affection**

Less talk, more action!

And what should you do if there are absolutely no problems in your marriage?

'I'd go right out and hire a private detective!

CHAPTER 2

Overcoming problems and worries without becoming demoralised

The ability to handle stress is one of the talents that can play a key role in helping you enhance the quality of your life. But even though it is of such crucial importance for success in life, it is amazing how few professions make the *ability to cope with stress and fear* key issues in their educational curricula and how little attention is paid to this objective in raising children and shaping their personalities.

The inability to cope with stress leads to demoralisation and paralysis. What each and every one of us needs is the ability to remain cool, calm and collected even while under great physical and psychological stress, to make the right decisions, to handle a huge workload and to stay in a good frame of mind.

Stress and worry are central elements of human existence. Worries are so ever-present that we simply have to learn to live with them, just as we have to learn to live with a husband or wife. Each and every one of us is so subject to stress and worry that we need principles of philosophy and of strategy, methods to preserve our working ability, our energy, our presence, our sense of what life is all about and our very personality in the face of this stress and worry.

In the future, working under pressure is going to be the normal state of affairs. Job pressures are going to be increasing. And this will also have an impact on our private lives. In the future, it will only be possible to achieve success in life if we are able to cope better with stress and maintain greater peace of mind.

The objective is clear: to cope with stress and worry without becoming demoralised and to attain a frame of mind that can best be described as 'cheerful peace of mind'.

Coping with stress and worry and not letting it demoralise you

1. **Physical strength**
2. **Mental energy**
3. **Appearance**
4. **Presence**

Frame of mind:

Cheerful peace of mind

We have to condition ourselves to chaos

Conditions are going to be changing at a faster pace in the future. The pendulum swings are going to be wider. Structures and environments will change. Governments, and along with them our laws, will be swinging from one extreme to the other from election to election.

The clarity, security and convenience of a social order that remains stable over long periods of time will no longer exist. The normal state of affairs will be rough seas. The ground on which we stand is going to become soft under our feet.

Chaos will become the normal state of affairs. Chaos is the collapse of order. Conditions will become less ordered. The exact opposite of a given situation will suddenly present itself. Changes will come crashing down upon us without any prior warning.

So we are going to have to learn to preserve our quality of life in situations that are characterised by chaotic events and a lack of continuity.

Chaotic times not only demand a greater ability to cope with stress, they also necessitate greater flexibility. Digging ourselves in is no help. The ability to change and respond is crucial, along with imagination and far-sightedness as prerequisites for taking preventative action.

We are going to have to learn to sit at a table of life that has uneven legs and that shakes with every move we make. Those who are able to enjoy their food of life undaunted will possess the genetic, philosophical and strategic foundation for these times.

They will know that they can expect no 'ordered conditions'.

Recognise the wisdom of an insecure life

Pay more attention to securing today's success and eliminating failures today instead of always focusing on achieving *absolute* security at some time in the future.

The only thing that is certain about the future is that it is uncertain. The motto for the future should be 'Happiness is the absence of unhappiness!' There is no such thing as long-term security: 'In the long run, we are all dead!'

But today is a different story. You can make today secure. As Charles Chaplin said: 'Happiness is a matter of organisation!' Of

The wisdom of an insecure life

Future:

Certain to be uncertain!

Today:

Can be made secure

Future:

'Happiness is the absence of

unhappiness'

Present:

'Happiness is a matter of organisation'

(and attention)

Over-insurance:

'Destroying the present in a vain attempt

to provide total security for the future'

course, happiness is more than that, but putting organisation and security into your todays plays a crucial role in the process.

The tomorrows will take care of themselves. This is the right approach. Every day represents a new beginning and a new opportunity.

Guard against the cardinal strategic mistake of 'over-insurance'

Over-insurance is the destruction of the present in the vain attempt to provide total security for the future. Don't ruin the present in favour of the future.

Don't live poorly today in the hope of a better future. Don't work yourself to death now so that you will be able to live well later. Have more compassion with yourself – right now! Don't chase after money with your health merely to have to chase after your health with your money later.

Don't set aside all of your reserves to secure your future. Free some reserves to secure your present, to keep your present from caving in. Don't fail in your present tasks, only because you don't want to free any resources from your strategic reserve to support your present offensive.

Reserves are not just intended for future catastrophes; they are also there to prevent catastrophes from happening in the present.

Don't only keep track of what you have achieved in the present. Every now and then, make a 'haven't done' list. In your marriage, don't neglect now what you want to do so far in the distant future. *The future is getting shorter with each passing year.*

Focus on living with an air of cheerful peace of mind

Don't view cheerful peace of mind and happiness merely as attitudes you should have, but as your life objectives. Life objectives are not just material results, they are also the way you live your life.

Draw up a list of those factors which have a positive influence on the quality of your life. Work on these factors. Don't focus on the negative; work creatively on methods and factors which will put you in a cheerful frame of mind.

Identify your key interests. Don't give up on them, and don't destroy them with suicidal loyalty. You aren't helping others by living your life through them.

Put a time limit on how long you are willing to live with stress factors

Don't be too proud of possessing exaggerated taker qualities. It would be absurd to concentrate only on cultivating a tremendous ability to cope with stress and leave matters at that. The ability to cope with stress is merely a precursor of decisively changing what can be changed. The ability to put up with things is the inability to change them. In this sense, patience is not a virtue; nor is the inability to become aggravated about certain stress factors a virtue. There is a form of peace of mind that is merely paralysis.

Problems don't solve themselves

Problems don't get any smaller by themselves. In many respects, it's later than you think. You're surrounded. You should have broken out long ago. You should have made a decision long ago. Now is the time to make it. Stop discussing it with others. Don't take on the mentality of a pendulum, swinging aimlessly back and forth between two goals until all of your strength has left you. Opt for one of the alternatives.

Don't confuse good will with action

Good will alone is not enough. Time and effort are not the desired result. The same old unsuccessful solutions to the same old problems won't get any better just because you keep repeating them over and over again.

Fundamental problems can't be solved with tactical means. Cosmetic touch-ups are no substitute when a problem requires major surgery.

Don't attribute difficulties to a lack of time. It is more likely that they are due to a lack of resolve and strength. What costs time is a lack of resolve and repeated half-hearted, unsuitable attempts.

Once you have made your decision, solving the problem will require only a fraction of the time you had thought.

Assess the situation

Don't shy away from the situation. Don't try to fool yourself. Don't make the situation look better than it really is. Don't become a champion of self-deceit.

Breaking out of the encirclement

- **It's later than you think!**
- **A decision is long overdue**
- **You are the one who has to make it**
- **Stop discussing it with others**

Alternative 1   **Alternative 2**

$$\longrightarrow$$
$$\longleftarrow$$
$$\longrightarrow$$
$$\longleftarrow$$

Pendulum!

Swinging aimlessly back and forth between two goals will sap all of your strength!

What you need is a diagnosis of stress. Stress is a mosaic. Stress diagnosis is already part of the therapy. Live by the philosophy that 'you should be your own audience!'

Identify the permanent stress factors in your life. Where are the bottlenecks, the sources of aggravation and the mistakes? What is it that is keeping your mind a prisoner and making a slave of you? What are the issues that are terrorising your state of mind?

Conserve your energy and add to it

Work out a programme for yourself to conserve your mental energy and add new energy to it.

Take steps to ensure that you are never depressed and fatigued at the same time. Sleep more during times when you are in a negative state of mind. During these phases, practise sound nutrition and engage in active sports. Your mental and physical strength hinge upon your health and fitness. And your ability to be decisive in doing the right things in your private and working life hinge upon your health and fitness.

There is virtually no other aspect in your life that you should come to grips with so intensively, creatively and systematically as with the task of conserving your health and fitness. They remain the keys to success in all of the other aspects of your life. Strive for a biological age that you could define as 'calendar age less 5'.

Don't take your work too seriously; but go about it seriously and professionally. Organise your work in such a way that it offers you relaxation, recharges your batteries and brings you happiness. This can be accomplished through a new style of cooperation, through a different type of communication, through work that is not hectic, through other work techniques and through a better work environment.

Don't view your work as effort and stress, but as a crucial instrument that you can employ to enhance your personal quality of life. Work serves not merely as a way to achieve material results. Work also demands a playful attitude. Constant analysis and training are necessary to arrive at methods that represent a synthesis between ease and professionalism.

Establish a style that suits you. Style is embossing your most inner self and your principles upon your behaviour patterns and actions. Style gives you inner tranquillity and peace of mind.

Expand your personal freedom

The fewer interrelationships you require, the more independent you are. What you need is a programme of independence.

Adapt your objectives to your time means. Don't overdo it when it comes to time. Straighten your battle lines. Before beginning a task, identify the amount of time it will require. Ask yourself whether the task and the objective it involves are really worth the time you will have to expend on them.

Bear in mind that it is not merely a question of time, but also a question of the demands that will be placed upon your strength reserves.

Concentrate on the vital factors. Don't spread yourself too thin. Quality is the supreme form of quantity. In life, it is quality that makes the difference. Focus on measures that will lead to qualitative expansion.

Give more thought to caution, far-sightedness and prevention. Don't plan away all of your resources. Keep your options open and retain some time reserves.

Don't ruin yourself by wanting to hold a position just in order to avoid having to admit 'defeat'.

Don't keep butting your head against the wall – the wall is harder.

You can only number among the elite if you straighten your battle line. This will provide you with the spearhead you need to advance deep into opportunity territory. Going into battle with a long front means that you will just barely have sufficient strength to make half a turn forward.

Make better use of the existing situation. Don't put at risk something that is going especially well. Don't strive for booty in a new endeavour at the risk of losing what you have just won.

Adapt your time to the objective you have selected. Guard against under-dosages. They make the enemy's forces even stronger.

Make sure your calendar contains time reserves. Establish a foundation for inner tranquillity by putting order into your personal affairs. How would these affairs have to look if you and the support you provide to your family and colleagues were no longer available to them tomorrow?

Which documents would have to be where? What about insurance and taxes? What instructions does your solicitor need? How do the documents have to be filed? Just which information would your

Strategy:

Selecting the right ship

Tactics:

Fighting over the best deck chair on the wrong ship.

Life =
buying goals with time

Art of living:
1. Tackling the right things
2. Not tackling the wrong things
3. Goals that are worth the effort
4. Less is more
5. Less will bring you more

Decisive non-doing

The key strategic question:
Why do it at all?

The key question to enthusiasts:
What will it get you?

Match your goals and tasks to the resources at your disposal

- Time
- Financial
- Physical
- Mental

Appropriate goals!

Use additional resources for bigger goals!

Phases of consolidation
Breaks to get yourself in shape again

Parting with things and doing without

- Ballast overboard
- Lighten load

'Giving up an untenable position numbers among the chief strategic achievements!'

- Fields of activity
- Partners
- Objects

It often costs more to part with things than it did to earn and acquire them in the first place!
Pay the price for your liberation – take the burden from your shoulders!

Your struggle for liberation

Holding on binds and destroys
- **Give up portions of the territory you have won**
  - **Shorten your battle line**
  - **Free up time capital**
- **Match objectives and tasks to your time resources**

Gain the time reserves you need to go on the offensive at promising points along the front

Don't spread it thin

↑ ↑ ↑ ↑ ↑ ↑ ↑ ↑

Hit hard

family need? Stipulate a security and convenience programme for your family and colleagues for this very sector.

Don't base all of your present decisions upon a future event that you're hoping for, looking forward to or striving for

Waiting for the big event in the future is the greatest destructor of your present quality of life. It is a very major impediment. It is waiting for clear, ordered conditions and the big solution to be served up on a silver platter.

One of the greatest strategic mistakes that can be made is the belief that there will be clear, convenient conditions at some time in the future and that it is unnecessary to create interim solutions now. *The belief in the existence of the perfect situation is one of the lowest rungs on the ladder of life experience.*

People with this belief shy away from the inconvenience of having constantly to shape new interim solutions. They find it all very unsatisfying. They are waiting for a great event that they hope will bring them total salvation and absolute freedom of action.

Every decision they make in the present is based upon their expectations for the future: 'We decided to buy a small house, because we know one day that our son will be moving out on his own!'

'How old is your son?' 'Well, Henry is three years old, but he's very big for his age!'

Don't allow negative past events to influence your present and future

End your past. Use sufficient resources to buy your freedom from the negative elements of your past.

Cast off the bonds that tie you to the negative aspects of the past. Don't become the victim of failure depression. *Only failures never fail – they say!*

Look ahead and make a new start without chains and bonds. You are going to be spending the rest of your life in the future!

Cardinal strategic error

Basing all present decisions upon a

desired

expected

coveted

event in the future

This phantom is the greatest destructor

of your present quality of life!

You never take the small steps that are

possible – because you're waiting for the

event that is to bring total salvation

The second choice

Perhaps, like many of us, you had long had a so-called 'first choice' in your life. This might have been a job, a profession or a personal relationship.

You spent an enormous amount of goodwill, attention, energy, time and thought attempting to make a success of this 'first choice'.

You exhausted yourself on your 'first choice'. You never got back what you put into it. All of your attention failed to get you very far. The less successful your efforts were, the more doggedly you struggled to achieve the coveted success. You struggled and never gave up. You kept on trying. You lived in a constant back-and-forth between distress and hope. In the end, though, in one way or another, you failed with your 'first choice'. Life with your 'first choice' was ended. Not by you, but by other people or events. For you, it was fate. You yourself would never have given up.

Then, along comes the opportunity of the 'second choice'. You have a new job. You enjoy your work. Your quality of life is high. Those around you are sincere and well-meaning. There are no intrigues. You enjoy great personal liberty, and you are independent.

You have every reason to be happy. But you're not; unfortunately, you once had that 'first choice'. Even years later, your thoughts continue to revolve around your failure with your 'first choice'. You are suffering from failure depression.

Since you are doing well at your 'second choice' anyway, you are putting only a fraction of the effort into it that used to be customary for your 'first choice'. Nevertheless, your 'second choice' is offering you everything you had wished for with your 'first choice'. You are merely insensitively viewing it as being a given. In the past, you would have done almost anything to wind up with only a fraction of what you now consider to be normal.

The thoughts that tie you to your 'first choice' apparently make it impossible for you to value and enjoy anything that is connected with the *success of failure*.

Think this analysis through, especially if your 'first choice' in-volved a personal relationship. These thoughts are of even greater significance here than in your work life. Here, too, cut the bonds that tie you to your 'first choice'. End your past. Your life is happening in the present and the future. Don't allow your successful 'second choice' to be destroyed by your failure with your 'first choice'.

Dedicate all of your energy, creativity and attention to your 'second choice'. In your present life, your 'second choice' is Number One! Guard against carelessness and neglect: 'Now that everything is wonderful, I don't have to give any more thought to it!'

Don't make excessive demands

It would be naive to wish that everything will go just as you would like it to. It is anything but normal for everything to go well. Be happy when it does. View it as a gift, not as a legal entitlement.

Don't wait for conditions to change. Conditions are almost always less favourable than you would like. But it is precisely these conditions that represent your point of departure. They form the frame of reference within which you have to live and work.

View problems as 'challenges', even if this word begins to sound funny. Sir Karl Popper, the philosopher, defines 'life' as the solving of problems. Problems are not the exceptions to the rule of life, they are the rule of life. Tackle problems with ease, without agitation, fear or panic.

Get to grips with the situation

When faced with unavoidable events and the blows that life deals, get to grips with the situation. Determine which aspects of a given situation can be changed and which can not.

Don't ponder the causes of the situation. Don't constantly dwell upon your own possible guilt.

Don't continually ask yourself what you should have done differently. No one on earth can always do what is right and best.

Concentrate on today

The burdens of today are easier to bear than anxiety about what might happen in the future.

So concentrate on today. Make it a successful day. Give it the concentration and attention it deserves as a single, independent day.

Free yourself of negative thoughts that focus on what you can't do or change today.

Don't allow the negative events in your past to influence your

- **present**
- **future**

Put an end to your past!

Look forward

→

New start

Coping with stress

- Get to grips with the situation
- Don't waste any thoughts on guilt
- Do what is in your power to combat stress

Contingency plans for future developments

Preventative organisational measures

'Today's burden is easier to bear than fearful thoughts about future developments!'

Concentrate totally on today. Don't burden today with the burdens of tomorrow!

Concentrate on the present moment

Now is the only point in time at which you can play an active role – right or wrong. Which is why now is the point in time that deserves the most attention from you.

If you perceive each instant, each moment, with intensity, you will be focusing all of your concentration into a tight laser beam.

You are vitally present. It's as if you were driving in a nail with a hammer. You wouldn't think of constantly looking to the left and right. It would be a shame for your thumb.

Many are filled with such inner agitation and panic that they are incapable of using all of their energy to concentrate on the present moment. They lead their lives with wavering eyes. Instead of concentrating on the point, they're always looking out of the corners of their eyes at either the past or the future.

They act like a floodlight, not a searchlight. They spread their energy too thin and thus reduce their success.

One of the prime rules of military strategy is 'Concentrate all of your forces on the crucial point!'

Only if you concentrate on the present moment will you be able to offer a partner the ultimate in quality attention. Only if you concentrate now on the present will you be able to listen. Only so will you have a real effect on others.

The ability to dedicate yourself totally to the present offers enormous advantages. It wipes away fear and anxiety. For you, all that exists now is the immediate moment. What happened before no longer bothers you. You are not constantly dwelling on what might possibly happen in the future. You don't allow your thoughts to hop around like scared rabbits. You are mentally disciplined.

By concentrating on the present, you pass on an enormous amount of strength to others. Your associates feel they have your full attention. They notice that you are there with them. This is what creates a charismatic personality. There can be no charisma without the ability to devote your complete attention to the present moment. It is impossible for you to project vitality if part of your energy is being sapped from the immediate present and put into the service of the past or the future.

If you succeed in concentrating on what demands your strength and attention now, you will be rewarded with inner tranquillity.

Nothing will escape you. You will be totally present. You will be

Pay attention to the present moment

Be a

laser beam

$\downarrow$

Bundled energy

Concentrated attention

Vital presence

acting professionally at this point in time. You will be avoiding mistakes and accidents. You will be there mentally, not just physically. If you do not succeed in concentrating on the present, you will be going through life like a zombie.

The intensity with which you live your life stems from the fact that you are totally there, even during the most minor activity. If you fail to respect the present, you will have no respect for your life.

Don't allow yourself to be paralysed by negative thoughts

No problem can be solved any easier by worrying. Worrying does not contribute to success. Constant worrying will not make you any stronger. Positive thoughts will. Worries have nothing to offer you.

Don't constantly dwell on events that you cannot change. You should stop mulling over what can't be changed. Take a clear philosophical position on these kinds of events and situations.

Don't worry prophylactically. Don't always be worrying about what might possibly happen. There are many creative people who destroy their quality of life for themselves and their families with anxious scenarios on the subject of 'what might possibly happen?'

Burdening yourself will not improve the situation. On the contrary!

Don't allow your imagination to put catastrophe into your mind set. Don't use your imaginative powers to dramatise the possible negative effects of a situation. All too often, the negative consequences you expected will never materialise, or their magnitude will in no way be commensurate with the anxiety you have suffered.

Control your thoughts. Negative thoughts will not change the situation. It is your task to transfer strength to others. So you must not allow negative thoughts to sap your own strength.

View difficulties and burdens as being a normal part of your life.

Here are some thoughts on the subject of 'worries and burdens' from President Richard Nixon's farewell to his cabinet and staff in Washington on 9 August 1974:

> Here is another one I found as I was reading, my last night in the White House, and this quote is about a young man. He was a young lawyer in New York. He had married a beautiful girl, and they had a lovely daughter, and then suddenly she died, and this is what he wrote. This was in his diary.
>
> He said, 'She was beautiful in face and form and lovelier still in

Has *any* difficulty ever been solved
because you worried about it or let it
spoil your frame of mind?

Schopenhauer:
Let not the fear of life spoil life and
its meaning

spirit. As a flower she grew and as a fair young flower she died. Her life had been always in the sunshine. There had never come to her a single great sorrow. None ever knew her who did not love and revere her for her bright and sunny temper and her saintly unselfishness. Fair, pure and joyous as a maiden, loving, tender and happy as a young wife. When she had just become a mother, when her life seemed to be just begun and when the years seemed so bright before her, then by a strange and terrible fate death came to her. And when my heart's dearest died, the light went from my life forever.'

That was Teddy Roosevelt in his twenties. He thought the light had gone from his life forever – but he went on. And he not only became president but, as an ex-president, he served his country, always in the arena, tempestuous, strong, sometimes wrong, sometimes right, but he was a man.

And as I leave, let me say, that is an example I think all of us should remember. We think sometimes when things happen that don't go the right way; we think that when we don't pass the bar exam the first time – I happened to, but I was just lucky; I mean, my writing was so poor the bar examiner said, 'We have just got to let the guy through.' We think that when someone dear to us dies, we think that when we lose an election, we think that when we suffer a defeat that all is ended. We think, as Teddy Roosevelt said, that the light had left his life forever.

Not true. It is only a beginning, always. The young must know it; the old must know it. It must always sustain us, because the greatness comes not when things go always well for you, but the greatness comes and you are really tested, when you take some knocks, some disappointments, when sadness comes, because only if you have been in the deepest valley can you ever know how magnificent it is to be on the highest mountain.

Don't just see the problems

Don't just register the difficulties, the impediments, the deficiencies and the mistakes. Why don't you take a look at what is going well and what you should be grateful for. Make a list of the positive things.

Have more compassion and indulgence with yourself. Why don't you see what you have accomplished, what you are and what you do for others. Take note of your own achievements. Be proud of your biography. Praise yourself for your achievements and reward yourself for them. Do more for yourself. Don't drive yourself so mercilessly. Stand next to yourself, smile at yourself, wink at yourself and laugh out loud together with yourself.

Don't just look at what you have *not yet* accomplished. Don't just look at your potential for achieving, which you 'unfortunately' have not yet fully tapped. Be happy that such a large supply of possibilities exists.

Let yourself be guided by the principle of a 'completionless life'. You will never be able to complete everything. You will never be finished. You will only be finished at the end of your way through life. There is no perfection along the way.

There is a difference between being professional and meticulous, on the one hand, and perfection on the other. What characterises perfection is that it is unattainable.

Nor, in this sense, are the burdens we have to bear perfect or final. These burdens are epochal in nature. Rest assured that every burden epoch will sooner or later come to an end. The tunnel does end somewhere.

As long as one of these epochs is ongoing, you can hardly imagine an end to it. You do not think it is possible that this problem could one day ever cease to exist.

There are situations where you wake up one morning and the problem has disappeared. Later, in retrospect, the burden you had to bear in the past seems to be covered by the fog of time.

Avoid panic and hysteria

Don't allow yourself to become agitated or toppled by trivial events. When these events arise, always remember that excitement and agitation only serve to multiply the 'coefficient of pettiness'.

Project calm serenity. Resolve not to be swept away by your emotions. Get upset less frequently. Eliminate frantic agitation from your behaviour.

Pay attention to your facial expression, your gestures and your manner of speaking. Speak more calmly, act more calmly and more deliberately.

Analyse your present burdens and worries

1.   What are they?
2.   What can you change about them right now?
3.   What can't you change about them right now?
4.   What can be changed when?

5.   What do you have to do to make the individual burdens easier to bear right now?

6.   What do you have to do to hasten the time when change will be possible?

7.   How can you use financial and other means to free yourself of the burdens and the worries more easily?

Do something about the things that are worrying you as soon as possible. Obtain the information that you need to view these factors in their proper perspective.

Cold-bloodedly and resolutely go about attacking the negative factors. Use the time you need, sufficient financial resources and competent support.

How you go about solving problems

Don't try to solve all of your problems at once. Work with a step-by-step plan. Delegate individual problems to others. There is even a special problem-solving industry: the legal profession.

Concentrate on one task. While performing this task, forget your other worries, problems and difficulties. Avoid special burdens, difficult work and discussing negative topics in the evening.

Put items that remind you of negative things out of your sight. Don't drag any ballast around with you. Lighten your load. Pay special attention to order, clarity and neatness.

Don't constantly dwell on this one negative stretch of your battle line. There are other parts of your battle line on which everything is going well. Make a mental visit to them every now and then. They are zones of recreation and relaxation.

Don't destroy the part of your battle line that is intact by allowing demoralising thoughts about the negative portion of the battle line to have a destructive effect on the positive zones. Concentrate on furthering what is going well. Don't allow it to fall into neglect because of one negative sub-zone.

Purge negative words and formulations from your vocabulary. There is a negative grammatical form for the future that is formulated: 'It's possible . . .' and a negative grammatical form for the past: 'We should have . . .'

Accustom yourself to using positive formulations. Cast off formulations with which you negatively label the content of what you

Put more emphasis on:

- **Your will to change**
- **Your ability to change**
- **Your power to change**
- **Your freedom to change**

Stop:

- **Tying yourself up**
- **Holding yourself back**
- **Paralysing yourself**

What can you totally change by yourself?
- ● **Right now**
- ● **Later**

What can you partially change by yourself?
- ● **Right now**
- ● **Later**

are going to say: 'It's possible; we should have; I fear that; I see a problem there; it'll never work; there's no point to it anyway!'

Don't constantly tell negative stories. Don't incessantly bemoan the negative situation and all of the problems that exist. Don't complain. Don't be reproachful. Don't gripe.

Talk is no substitute for action

Finally, make the necessary decision and pursue it with resolve. Don't shy away from a decision just because every possible solution also involves negative consequences. In this world, there are no solutions that have only positive effects.

What looks like a huge mountain of work in front of you isn't really a mountain, it's a mirage. This mountain has nothing to do with work. Although it looks like a *mountain of work*, in reality it's a *valley of decisions*.

Once you have made the necessary decision, the mountain of work will turn into a gentle hill. So don't try to fool yourself into believing that a huge job is awaiting you and only a lack of time is preventing you from levelling the mountain. This kind of comment is merely an excuse and an alibi.

It's not a lack of time that is preventing you from solving the problem. It's a lack of resolve. Taking a resolute step in the right direction is half the task of mastering the work.

Keep your momentum up. Don't let burdens paralyse you. Get up and get moving. Work. Activity and concentration will take your mind off negative things.

The term clever conjures up unpleasant associations. It is like driving a car round a bend on two wheels. But it is possible that there is an end that justifies the means. *There is one task* for which you can never be 'clever' enough. This is the task of being cheerful. This task is worthy of all of your resources.

What is it that suddenly has a positive effect on your state of mind? Which people are able to accomplish this? Which activities put you in the right frame of mind?

What you need is a policy of active mood management. Your mood, your frame of mind, gives you the strength and vigour to overcome obstacles. You'll learn the individual steps that you can undertake to put you in a positive frame of mind and keep you there in Chapter 3, on the 'anti-aggravation system'.

During periods of heavy burdens and stress, free yourself of all obligations that are not absolutely necessary. During these times, in particular, learn to say no with resolve. During these kinds of periods, avoid all unnecessary changes in your work routine and your routine environment.

Mobilise your time and strength reserves to combat the burdens that are facing you. During these periods, stop trying to be a part of everything and trying to be everywhere.

Concentrate on the few activities that are vital and forget about the many that are trivial. If you fail to do so, you will be left with neither the time nor the strength to break down the roadblocks that exist right now.

Strive to improve your physical fitness

Set up a weekly programme for doing this. The more you are physically able to handle, the more you will be able to bear emotionally.

Eat according to a plan and more slowly. Get enough sleep. Exercise to relax. Consult your doctor and listen to his or her advice.

In providing yourself with strength and the right frame of mind, start at the periphery. Work positively from the outside in. Dress with the utmost care. Go to a better hair stylist. Improve your complexion. A tanned face looking back at you from the mirror has less of a worrisome and demotivating effect.

Use the power of music to improve your frame of mind. Do more things that you personally enjoy doing.

During worrisome situations, pay particular attention to order, clarity and neatness. These are the times when discipline in superficial things takes on great importance.

Which people and activities motivate you?

Draw up a list of the people and activities that have a significantly motivating effect on you. Pay more attention to those people and activities.

Don't begrudge yourself breaks and luxuries. Treat yourself to a massage, have a facial.

Do it all without any pangs of conscience. The people you like won't benefit if you don't feel well. And the people you don't like shouldn't have the pleasure of knowing that you don't feel well.

Day in and day out, train yourself to enjoy cheerful peace of mind. Don't always ask yourself what could possibly happen to you. Spend more time thinking about how much you can do to combat the obstacles and difficulties.

The principle of grand strategy is 'In the long run, nothing counts – absolutely nothing!' Although this might sound like resignation, it is nevertheless true. It is the principle of human existence.

Hold back

Keep your obligations to a minimum. Stipulate principles of *contact strategy*. Under a contact strategy, you question the meaningfulness and intensity of partnerships.

Steer clear of certain people. Make a list of unnecessary contacts that offer you nothing in return besides meaningless, burdensome obligations. Do not allow yourself to be forced into obligations. These attempts are more often than not made with subversion than with coercion.

Don't pile burdens upon yourself that are the result of incorrectly chosen partnerships.

Make a wide berth around promising projects which, it is said, can be handled on the side, without any major effort on your part. There is no such animal. Experience shows: 'What you can earn on the side without any effort or expense on your part will cost you the most later on!' Anyone who promises you major success without any effort or burdens on your part is a scoundrel, and is usually much more than that.

Don't mix as much. Withdraw instead of trying to be everywhere. Delegate more. Don't feel that you are responsible for everything. Don't assume total responsibility for the Planet Earth.

Study your notebooks and records from past years. Then you will suddenly remember all of the forgotten worries and burdens of days gone by. You will remember the fears you had and the emotional situation in which you found yourself.

You will find textbook examples of how senseless it is to drive yourself crazy over burdens and worries, to panic and to spoil your frame of mind. What you are going through right now will probably pale in the light of what you have already put behind you.

If you are presently struggling with a major obstacle, there is a strong desire to find a countermeasure that is just as powerful. But

One obstacle

Wanted: one countermeasure

◀ **?**

One obstacle

Possible: a mosaic of action

◀

Tiny bits and pieces of diligence and ideas!

this will virtually never be possible. The obstacle is on one side of the balance scale, but the *one* big counterweight you are seeking for the other side of the scale does not exist. The only possibility that is left to you is a *mosaic of action*. The key to the solution is, as always, tiny bits and pieces of diligence and ideas.

Let friends help you

Burdens are easier to bear with the help of friends. It is friends who help you bear and overcome the bad hands that fate has dealt you. Friends can bring you across the bridge to the other shore and help you heal your wounds.

Friends can use the right words to bring you back from your state of pure emotionality and return to you the ability to think in rational terms. Friends can improve your basic state of mind and free you of your fixation on your worries.

In this sense, friends are every bit as important as life insurance. Keep this in mind and carefully cultivate your relations with your friends. At work, it is on the interpersonal level that we first begin to recognise the importance of a professional view of functions. 'Interpersonal relationship cultivation management' is the generic name for this.

CHAPTER 3

The Gross system for combating stress

Conserving your frame of mind and mental energy

You'll recall 'Success in life is what you feel and think.'

What you feel and think depends upon the way in which you handle your personal resources. If you are faced by a constant shortage of resources, you will not be as happy as if you had sufficient reserves at your disposal. This is a truism.

The resources that immediately come to mind are financial means and time. They are important factors in your personal and professional success. They are also the crucial resources to which all of us give so much thought. We do a great deal of thinking about how to ensure that financial means, in particular, are properly employed.

We possess a comprehensive repertoire of principles, methods and tools for handling money and time. We have at our disposal financial-planning and time-planning methods. We have security systems that prevent our time and our money from simply slipping through our fingers senselessly and unnoticed.

The situation is entirely different in the case of two further types of resources that are at least as important for our success in life as money and time. These resources are *your mental energy* and *your frame of mind*.

No one would sit back and carelessly allow money or time to wither away; but very few seem to care about their mental energy and frame of mind. When it comes to these two factors, most of us are possessed by an inconceivable degree of inactivity and fatalism.

This is probably because we have an insufficient awareness of the need for taking decisive action here, too, and we lack a well-founded understanding about the power that these two factors represent.

Daily aggravation numbers among the greatest destructors of your mental energy and your frame of mind. This is where you should start. As an aid in achieving this objective, this chapter describes an anti-aggravation system that functions extremely well. It is a system for your personal mood management. Mood management means actively fostering and conserving your frame of mind.

The daily losses from which your frame of mind suffers are not brought about by events that have the proportions of major catastrophes. It is minor occurrences, frequently of ridiculously small proportions, that suddenly kill your mood.

Take a look at the mood swing of someone who wants to staple together several sheets of paper and suddenly notices that the stapler is empty. Some people give the impression that, when an impediment of this type suddenly occurs, it is capable of bringing them to the verge of a nervous breakdown. They virtually go into shock.

It is always the same or similar events that affect your frame of mind. It is not a selection of fatal risks, it is the many small impediments, bothers and troubles. It's not the landslide, it's the banana peels on the path you use every day.

The essence of human beings, their basic frame of mind, as well as their appearance, is affected not so much by major catastrophes as by the inability to provide themselves with a philosophy and a system for avoiding aggravation and for wisely handling the aggravation that cannot be avoided.

If you want to be successful in shaping your life, and to a great extent this means your frame of life, if you want to avoid being gradually ground down by the events of individual days over the course of time, if you don't want to soil the meaning of life, you need a system for coping with aggravation.

Aggravation is an ever-present threat. It is a companion you have to learn to handle and to live with. Aggravation must be tackled just as professionally as the tasks and challenges of your work.

You have to unearth systematically the causes of aggravation. Simply being able to recognise the causes that trigger aggravation within you will provide you with ideas for reaching a higher level of mood-impairment avoidance.

By researching and alertly observing the causes of aggravation, you will come to recognise where you have thus far not been shaping your life as well as you could, what you are handling unprofessionally and what is hindering you. You will see what you are lacking in terms of basic decision-making skills, behaviour patterns, prevention, planning, organisation and tools.

The anti-aggravation system will not only aid you in becoming more cheerful and relaxed, it will also help you become more professional. This system is based upon the following underlying concept: up until now, aggravation has been directed against you; now you are going to turn the tables and put aggravation in your service. Up until now, you were the errand-runner for your aggravation; now, aggravation will become your assistant.

In other words, you will be acting in accordance with one of the most successful strategies in this field: 'The exact opposite is correct!'

The anti-aggravation system conditions you to go on the offensive, to take action.

If you want to avoid aggravation in the future and respond to aggravating events differently from the way you have in the past, you will have to establish yourself on a different frame-of-mind plane, which wil unleash many times your present implementation energy.

As your aggravation increases, it turns you into a different person. Of course, the same also holds true when your aggravation decreases. You might even turn into the kind of person you once used to be.

This could very well bring more happiness than anything else to you yourself, to your partner, to your children and to your associates at work.

You will hardly be able to believe it. All of a sudden, you will once again be a person who is not constantly under pressure, irritable, nervous and worried.

Less aggravation means less unrest and less rushing. You have fewer fears and fewer worries. Aggravation, on the contrary, almost always triggers fears. Something happened, so there are bound to be negative consequences. 'What's going to happen as a result of this? How's this going to affect certain relationships? What's this going to do to my reputation?'

If you handle aggravation correctly, you will have available to you a selection of positive primary and secondary effects. One of the primary effects is that you will conserve your energy and your state of mind. The positive secondary effects include a reduction in the volume of your fears.

One hour of intensive aggravation costs you more energy than twelve hours of hard work. This is fatal, because there are enough drains on your mental energy to begin with. Many people want a piece of your energy. Many people eat away at your stock of energy.

There are two groups of people: the givers and the takers. Many believe that successful personalities are characterised by the fact that they 'have and take'. However, it is much more likely that their special character trait is that they 'give'.

Let's summarise the point of departure; it is important enough. There is not the least doubt that you need a programme for conserving your energy. From now on, you simply have to avoid unnecessary energy losses.

The main reason for your personal energy crisis is the constant presence of aggravating events. Aggravation not only robs you of your energy and your frame of mind, it also poses a real threat to your health, destroys your vitality, steals your human spark and reduces you to the level of a disciplined robot.

Perhaps you not only have objectives at work; perhaps you also have goals that relate to your vitality, your physical strength and your mental state. Perhaps your objective is: 'biological age = calendar age minus five years.' If so, the anti-aggravation system can provide you with an instrument that will help you achieve this objective.

Aggravation is like swallowing poison

Aggravation is mood suicide. If you get aggravated daily, you are drinking a hydrochloric acid cocktail daily. Aggravation produces unbelievable effects. It is amazing what a modest little negative spark can accomplish. A mouse gives birth, and a mountain is born. An effect with minimal value can keep a human being breathless all day long. All it takes is the creative ugliness of a certain arch enemy.

An apparently unimportant barb, delivered within the space of five seconds by a professional purveyor of caustic remarks, can make the recipient incapable of working productively for two whole hours.

Aggravation acts in all directions. It is a cluster bomb that leaves behind an impressive array of consequences.

The heat losses that are caused by aggravation are enormous. Imagine the energy that you could save both at home and at work, if you were only able to get the daily aggravation out of your life.

How would you be towards those who are closest to you? What could you do for your quality of life if you yourself became aggravated less often?

Viewed from this perspective, it is simply inconceivable why so

Aggravation

is like swallowing poison

Mood suicide on the instalment plan

Your daily hydrochloric acid cocktail

many people still continue to allow themselves to be poisoned anew day in and day out. And the poisoning should be taken literally. Just think of the shot of adrenaline that aggravation sends into your biological system.

Aggravation paralyses you. Curare, the poison used by the Amazon Indians on their arrows, is child's play by comparison. Among the poison arrows of the world, aggravation *reigns supreme*.

Aggravation destroys your ability to work and achieve. It prevents you from getting ahead and makes it more difficult for you to achieve your objectives.

The only time you feel relaxed and content is when you are getting ahead with your work. But aggravation lets mountains of work pile up. Aggravation thus creates your main stress factor: 'unfinished work'.

Aggravation robs you of your presence. No one who is aggravated possesses charisma. Charisma can exist only if you are cheerful and at ease, if you are at peace within and if you act from within. Aggravation gets you going, but the wrong way. Aggravation robs you of your festive radiance and reduces you to the brightness of an emergency exit light in a basement corridor. It generates pessimism and robs you of your independence to act.

Aggravation is a fashion designer who specialises in pettiness instead of petticoats. Aggravation weaves a negative pattern. It causes you to act in a manner that is detrimental to your reputation.

Aggravation makes it more difficult for you to lead, encourage and provide support to others.

How can you expect to get others moving if aggravation is dragging you down like the concrete around the feet of a former Mafia member?

Aggravation robs you of your inner tranquillity

Aggravation lowers your irritation threshold. It ensures that minor events will have an easier time toppling you. It narrows your awareness and makes you short-sighted or blind. It reduces your judgement, causes you to make errors and spawns new aggravation.

Aggravation distracts you

Aggravation makes you nervous, flustered and volatile. It takes away your concentration and steals from you the strength for relaxed communication.

Aggravation makes you undisciplined. It robs you of your view for priorities, rankings and differences in significance.

You become the object of emotions. You march off without any thought and without any planning. Aggravation drops you from the soccer team and degrades you to being the ball. Aggravation kicks you and chases you across the playing field. Aggravation turns human beings into puppets.

Aggravation forces the blood out of your brain and into your muscles

So all of a sudden you can make enormous leaps. But you don't know where to leap. Your mind lacks the capacity to plan. You are moving forcefully, but without purpose or direction.

Aggravation robs you of your time

You explode and then sometimes need hours to collect yourself, to gather your composure again. Aggravation leaves you with no time, no attention and no energy to do the really important things today. Aggravation isolates you from the significant things. It demolishes your schedule for the whole day.

Aggravation robs you of your cheerfulness

Aggravation takes from you what makes human beings different from animals. It makes you vicious.

Analyse how your frame of mind develops

Draw up a statement of profit and loss with respect to your frame of mind. Your frame of mind, like money, is in short supply. And a good frame of mind is often in even shorter supply.

Think about how important accounting is when it comes to your financial resources. There is an enormous repertoire of principles, methods and tools that are employed to monitor the flows of money.

But there is also an instrument with which you can monitor which way your frame of mind is flowing. It is this instrument that we now want to discuss.

Each of us knows that lost time can never be recovered. But neither can a lost frame of mind. Along with it, a part of your life has been irretrievably lost.

There is no insurance company that will offer to replace losses that you have suffered in your frame of mind. Had you taken out 'anti-aggravation insurance', you would be receiving cheques from your insurance company every day. This alone would lift your spirits. And one day, you would be in such an outstanding frame of mind that you would no longer be able to file any new claims. Then you would become aggravated again and you'd find yourself in a truly 'fortunate' situation.

You need a frame-of-mind balance sheet

Use a balance sheet to realise how many hours a day and how many days a month you are cheerful, happy and relaxed. Do you know how many days a month you are actually free of unrest, hurry, aggravation, fears and worries?

View your frame of mind as being your assets. Look at aggravation as liabilities. How high is your indebtedness?

Equating aggravation with liabilities is by no means far-fetched. Almost always, aggravation serves as your negative link with other people and with other things.

Doing senseless things

Let's analyse further the destructive effects of aggravation. Aggravation drives you to do senseless things. Take a look at your diary for last year. Study how you used your time.

You will recognise how many bad time investments, bold and destructive offensives and purposeless battles were triggered by aggravation.

Aggravation makes you aggressive

Aggravation leads you to wound others. Aggravation makes you unjust and aggressive. When you are aggravated, you attack, strike back, accuse, hurt and threaten.

Frame-of-mind balance sheet

How many hours a day ☐

How many days a week ☐

Are you cheerful, happy and at ease?

Free of unrest, hurry, aggravation,

fears, worries?

Aggravation helps you create enemies and weakens your position. Aggravation helps you breed further aggravation.

Aggravation costs money

An analysis of the costs that are caused by the factor of aggravation in an organisation would unearth amazing results.

Aggravation causes you to lose orders, customers and staff. Aggravation causes you to lose time and money:

1.   How much paid working time is lost per day as a result of aggravation?
2.   How much time is devoted to infighting within your organisation as a result of aggravation?
3.   How many projects are hindered and slowed down?
4.   How many letters are written, how many telephone calls made because of aggravating events?
5.   How much time is lost in handling complaints?

For over ten years, the medical director of a hospital was engaged in a power struggle with a colleague. This power struggle had been poisoning the lives of both. Their work was no longer uppermost in their minds; it was handled as a matter of routine. Aggravation about the existence of the other was uppermost in the mind of each.

One day, one of the two took sick and was admitted to the hospital. That evening, he found on his night-stand a huge bouquet of flowers from his arch enemy. Attached to the bouquet was a note: 'My dear colleague, What on earth do you think you're doing? Hurry up and get well. We need you!'

The recipient of this missive was touched to tears. Later, he said: 'Actually, I had known for the whole ten years that my colleague is really one of the most exceptional and lovely people on earth!'

What a negative art of wasting life! The lives of two human beings were poisoned for years. Only because neither of the two had mastered the 'art of making peace'.

Let's return to the costs of aggravation. There is virtually no other cost-reduction measure that can produce such enormous results as the elimination of aggravation in businesses and other organisations.

In the personal sector, eliminating or reducing aggravation brings about a totally different married and family life.

Aggravation drives you into senseless obligations

Aggravation sends you on your way with a tremendous kick in the pants. The true kick-off meeting is when a human being and aggravation come face to face.

Following an aggravating situation, you immediately contact others. You find the situation in which the aggravation has put you to be intolerable. You promise unreasonably high compensation to others if they will only help you in your present situation.

You forget your reserve. Aggravation robs you of your caution. You reveal yourself to others to a degree that would be inconceivable if your mind were clear.

You reveal secrets. You carelessly comment about others. What you voice puts you in the hands and in the power of others.

You speak with totally unsuitable partners about topics you should never be discussing with them.

Aggravation is the enemy of aesthetics

Aggravation produces horrible faces. It purses your lips, makes your face stony and your stomach sour. It reduces the space between your neck and your collar and it plays havoc with your appearance.

Aggravation is an infectious disease

It doesn't take long until everybody is aggravated. It's as if the entire organisation had come down with scabies. Employees who are aggravated shovel their aggravation on to your customers.

There is a law that is called the 'disproportionate transmittal of a bad frame of mind'.

Customers refuse to stand for this negative behaviour. They complain and return the aggravation. In many organisations, there is a vicious cycle of aggravation.

Highly qualified people are especially susceptible to aggravation

This group includes the creative minds and the professionals. They have more antennae, consequently they receive more stimuli. They have a better feel for the difference between what should be and what is.

Aggravation

forces the blood out of your brain and

into your muscles

Attack or flee . . .

Aggravation

- **Destroys your frame of mind**
- **Paralyses you**
- **Makes it impossible for you to achieve**
- **Distracts you**
- **Narrows your awareness**
- **Makes you undisciplined**
- **Drives you to do senseless things**
- **Steals your time**
- **Spawns new aggravation (recycles the aggravation)**

The aggravation syndrome

- Pursed lips
- Corners of the mouth
- Yellowish complexion
- Tight collar
- Sour stomach
- Bitter taste
- Stony face
- Poisoned thoughts

Not a pretty picture – not a good example!

Anti-aggravation system

↓

Mood management

The lazy, the dilettantes and the self-satisfied are less susceptible to aggravation. They are much more frequently the source of the aggravation and much less frequently its victim.

People who have long enjoyed nothing but success are especially susceptible to stress and threatened by aggravation. Even small set-backs depress them far out of proportion. They lack experience in coping with set-backs. They are not used to being in negative situations that often.

Others have an easier time of it there. They have had virtually no positive achievement experiences. All their lives they have been in a way cheerfully moving from one set-back to another. They are an aggravation-resistant breed. They are the natives of Flop City.

The big-mouths who have settled in the suburbs of the political landscape are also less sensitive to aggravation.

Their distorted personality traits and their ambitious nature would appear to be resistant even to aggravation.

Aggravation prefers people who are well-mannered. They are the ones it attacks. People who are well-mannered need the anti-aggravation system. People with no manners do not need it. They possess natural immunity.

What kinds of aggravation have you already been putting up with for much too long?

Certain kinds of aggravation are so ever-present that you may have lost the ability to wonder about them. This type of aggravation is simply accepted as being unavoidable. It has become routine. What counts when dealing with the causes of these types of aggravation is: 'It takes a bit of ingenuity to recognise what is so obvious!'

In dealing with this type of aggravation, you have to regain your ability to wonder how you could have simply accepted it for so long.

Over the course of the years, certain little monkeys that have been hopping about on your shoulders day in and day out have become a normal part of your life. Sooner or later, it will be high time for you to view this normal state of affairs as being an intolerable situation.

If the same old aggravation song is being played on the radio every day, it will eventually turn into an aggravation hymn. Don't let that happen.

Which impediments, mistakes and set-backs occur time and time again? What aggravates you, your family and your customers or

You've been putting up with certain causes of aggravation for much too long!

What causes aggravation or is involved with it?

1. **Which events?**
2. **Which behaviour on your part?**
3. **Which behaviour on the part of others?**
4. **Which people?**
5. **Which activities?**
6. **Which equipment?**

Change them?
Get rid of them?
Replace them?

colleagues time and time again? Find out by performing a thorough aggravation diagnosis.

Which persons trigger aggravation time and time again? Which kinds of aggravation do you yourself cause? Where are the special risk factors in your private and working lives? Which weaknesses, bottlenecks and sources of loss produce aggravation?

Let your partner, your children and your staff at work help you in identifying these risk factors.

What do you lose every day?

How much joy, energy, drive, time and money does aggravation take from you day in and day out?

Conserve your energy. Cultivate a greater sense of responsibility towards yourself. Increase the expectations that you place upon your state of mind. Don't destroy yourself by constantly being worried and aggravated. The time to put an end to the aggravation is today, this very minute.

Utilise generous portions of the means at your disposal to eliminate the primary causes of your aggravation. Make time and money available for this purpose. Buy your freedom from the permanent sources of your aggravation.

Nurses in a doctor's office complained to their boss that several patients were especially unfriendly. He analysed the situation and found that only very few patients were involved. But the aggravation-producing behaviour of these people was all that was needed to destroy the atmosphere in his practice for hours on end.

The doctor decided to invite the worst offenders to an 'exit interview'. Displaying a complete understanding of their personalities and being as friendly as possible to them, he advised these patients to seek out another physician. What he did not reveal to them was the fact that this other physician was his prime competitor.

The thought that a troupe of aggravation producers would soon be plying their trade at his colleague's practice provided a tremendous boost to this physician's spirits. We have here a good example of an especially effective, and of course extremely considerate and well-mannered, anti-aggravation campaign.

If you want to free yourself of aggravation, you will have to make an investment or a sacrifice. It doesn't always have to be much. But eventually you have to decide to do it. Don't wait any longer. Find

STOP ⟶ Goal

↓

Aggravation

**Aggravation results when you want to
attain a goal and are prevented from
doing so:**

You'll have to wait

The number is busy

The flight is delayed

The things aren't ready yet

He's not there

We're closed for the holidays

There's no taxi available

out how much you will have to pay to rid yourself of the aggravation. And then pay the price, because you've suffered long enough from certain types of stress and aggravation.

A huge reward for successful anti-aggravation measures

You will once again become a wellspring of optimism. You will become younger. You will become happier. You will regain your cheerful peace of mind.

All at once, you will have more energy. You will be less paralysed. You will enjoy your work more. People who are successful and passionate in their work view work as a hobby. But it can only remain a hobby if the negative circumstances that go with it are kept to a minimum. Expressed differently: your work is your hobby, but there are limits. The limits are determined by the volume of aggravation that this work involves, and of course by such other factors as lack of time.

If there are fewer sources of aggravation, there are fewer hot tempers. You will get along better with others. You will eliminate friction. You will produce a better atmosphere of cooperation.

All of a sudden, you will find that you possess a new reservoir of strength for getting ahead. You will gain the ability to implement necessary changes. You will be able to act in a considered, professional manner. And this will apply to both your working and private lives.

Continue your aggravation analysis

1. What aggravates you virtually every day?
2. What disturbs you, irritates you and destroys your frame of mind?
3. What paralyses and depresses you?
4. What prevents you from getting ahead faster?

Write down a list of which kinds of aggravation exist because of which relationships and ties and would probably no longer be there if these relationships and ties did not exist.

Benefits of the anti-aggravation system

- More cheerful
- More creative
- More energy
- Better appearance
- More at ease
- More aggressive
- More presence
- Health

Anti-aggravation system

Clears the way

Lets you get ahead without interference

System for managing your personal resources

Time

Health

Mental energy

Frame of mind

Drive

Appearance

Which kinds of aggravation result almost automatically from the nature of your profession?

1.   Which kinds of aggravation are related to your level in the organisational hierarchy?
2.   Which kinds of aggravation exist because you are especially successful in a given field and have a lead over the others?
3.   Which kinds of aggravation result from the kinds of achievements you have had?
4.   Which kinds of aggravation result from the way you live and from where you live?

Every profession comes with its own specific type of aggravation

Every profession and every job involves specific types of aggravation. This is a fact that you have to acknowledge. Specific aggravation belongs to any given profession, just as much as the name of the profession or the specific education and training that are required for this profession.

It is not very productive to get upset constantly about the aggravation that is inherent to a given profession. You have to assume that every profession is surrounded by a special breed of aggravation wolves.

You can resign yourself to the fact that these wolves are gradually moving in on you. But it is much better to develop powerful means of prevention and response that will force the aggravation wolves to keep at bay.

One of Germany's most successful convention and congress organisers is constantly being visited by aggravation, because every time he puts on a convention or congress his less successful competitors try to steal his mailing lists and the names of his carefully selected speakers.

There are two alternatives for dealing with this type of behaviour: either to repeatedly become aggravated about it or sooner or later to decide to view this situation as being the price that simply has to be paid for success.

You have to come to realise that the reward for success cannot always be a positive one. The successful are rewarded with higher tax brackets.

People who are especially successful need bodyguards. They provide physical protection. What is needed now are bodyguards to protect against aggravation.

Your anti-aggravation list

The anti-aggravation list is one of the most productive tools in your programme to liberate yourself from aggravation. Its mere existence in your immediate vicinity demonstrates to you the fact that aggravation would like nothing better than to be a normal part of your life and work.

One source of aggravation after another emerges in front of you. Over the course of the day, the aggravation grows to become a complete band of thieves.

Each kind of aggravation enters your life and, grinning shamelessly, waits to see what is going to happen to you now or what you are now going to do to yourself.

Suppose that you simply ignore the aggravation. That you refuse to let yourself by affected by it. Then you could look the aggravation in the eye and say *Rien ne va plus!*

Place the anti-aggravation list in front of you on your desk. When people enter your office, first look them over calmly and then add their name to the list, whose title should be written in letters large enough so that it is clearly visible to them: 'Anti-aggravation list'.

Of course, it is not necessary to go to this extreme; but it would be conceivable. Seriously, though, write down the true sources of aggravation. Every time something happens, ask yourself what you would have to do now to ensure that this kind of aggravation can no longer occur in the future.

Fortunately, it is very difficult to find the kind of aggravation against which there are no preventative defences. You will come to see that you will come up with an idea for a preventative solution, with a different attitude or with a different response to virtually every kind of aggravation.

But you will also be amazed at how many causes you will have to add to your list during the course of a morning. This shows how far removed you often still are from preventative defences and which possibilities are open to you for reaching a higher plane of circumspection and organisation.

What could also happen, of course, is that you have the anti-

The five biggest aggravations

What worries you?

What disturbs you?

What holds you back?

What aggravates you time and

time again?

1. _____

_____

2. _____

_____

3. _____

_____

4. _____

_____

5. _____

_____

aggravation list on the desk in front of you and nothing happens. At nine o'clock, you still have no idea about what to add to the list. At ten o'clock there has still been no aggravation. Now that's really aggravating!

When you read through your anti-aggravation lists several weeks later, you will recognise the following: the individual aggravation that upset you so much a while ago has long since been neutralised; it no longer holds any power over you and does not have the least emotional effect on you.

This is not merely because time has passed since the aggravation. Another reason could be that many other kinds of aggravation have long since neutralised the earlier one. The law that applies here is 'Greater aggravation makes smaller aggravation disappear!'

You will also recognise that the spectrum of aggravation is truly impressive. You will see that aggravation is waiting to pounce on you during every activity, every time you do a job and every time you deal with someone.

The most positive realisation for you will be that, with your tubulation of aggravation, you will have a wealth of ideas available to you, probably greater than anything you would be able to discover using so-called 'creative methods'. The anti-aggravation list is simply the *supreme list of ideas*.

Don't just keep your own anti-aggravation list. Ask your staff to do the same. With the results of these observations, you will have the foundation for taking a different approach in motivating your staff.

The normal, conventional approach to motivating staff is to ask 'What can we offer our employees in the way of incentives and rewards?'

The approach made possible by keeping an anti-aggravation list, on the contrary, is 'What can and must we prevent, eliminate or change in order to stop our employees from being *demotivated*?'

At home, you can use the same principles that have just been described for your work. Encourage your partner and children to list their aggravation.

Make a game of it. Call each kind of aggravation a land mine. You and your family will then be acting as a mine-sweeping squad. The anti-aggravation list serves as the detection system for finding the mines that have always been exploding in your faces. If you employ the system that has been described here, there will be fewer explosions in your family.

Anti-aggravation list

No.	Date	Aggravation	How to avoid in future?

© Guenter F. Gross, Munich

Avoiding aggravation

The best way to cope with aggravation is to prevent it from ever occurring. Practise careful and alert aggravation prophylaxis. Use checklists. You need checklists for all types of tasks, such as trips, conferences, meetings and other work.

The checklists contain the risk factors that could produce aggravation in connection with these activities. You then automatically eliminate the risk factors.

Decide to bring about a permanent change in your frame of mind. You can opt for peace of mind. You can begin peace of mind. Gain more peace of mind. Institute a philosophy of tranquillity. Programme yourself for the positive mode. Desensitise yourself.

In particular, organise yourself better; and do it in your private life as well. It was with good reason that Charles Chaplin said: 'Happiness is a matter of organisation!'

Of course, happiness involves more than just good organisation. But this will produce a great many results.

Don't destroy a single day

Don't say that any single day is a 'bad' day: 'This is another bad day today!' Don't do that to the day. Don't defame it. Don't malign its honour. Fight for the right of happiness to which every day is entitled.

Instead, observe what others want to do to this unique day, which will never come again: 'Another attempt to assassinate my day!' Don't forget that it is your unique day, and that it will never return again!

Observe the development of your frame of mind

Pay more attention to the development of your frame of mind. Register any increase in nervous irritability. You can tell partners that you happen to be especially irritable right now. Merely by voicing this fact, you will reduce your irritability. Irritability does not like to be recognised and spoken to directly.

Withdraw for a while when your irritability increases. Put yourself in quarantine to avoid infecting those around you. Give yourself a chance to cool down.

Aggravation proportions

How often do these kinds of aggravation occur?

Per day   ☐

Per week   ☐

Per month   ☐

How many people act this way?

One out of   10   ☐

One out of   100   ☐

One out of 1,000   ☐

Today's aggravation

What?	Causes?	How to avoid in future?

Today's positive things

_____

_____

_____

A well-known entrepreneur had a chin-up bar installed in his office. Whenever he noticed that one of his executives was becoming increasingly irritable, he politely asked him to do a few chin-ups.

Many of his executives were overweight. That made it all the more difficult for them. Their irritability was quickly transformed into a lack of breath. That provided the entrepreneur with an additional benefit. He could then continue the planned dialogue in the form of a monologue. That's how easy life can be if a suitable instrument is available.

Don't aggravate yourself prematurely

Don't aggravate yourself prophylactically. You're awaiting a negative event. You expect someone else's attitude towards you to be negative. The exact opposite then happens. You expect hindrance and resistance and get the green light and open arms.

What a pity for all that wonderful aggravation beforehand! What a pity for the hours that you sat in bed at night coming up with scenarios and revelling in fantasies of revenge! Now there's no occasion to put them to use, no opportunity for revenge. What a tragedy!

The president of a company and a sales manager were preparing to call on a customer who had been spoiling their moods for months. There was nothing about them or the company that pleased the customer, who bought very little and criticised everything.

After giving a good deal of thought to the matter, the two decided to terminate the association. This decision cheered them up.

They had carefully prepared the scenario for their approach. They would calmly listen to the customer's laments, nodding approvingly. They would concur, and then they would say: 'We understand you very well. We admire your experience and your good judgement, and we would like to make a proposal to you that will undoubtedly meet with your approval. Your analysis of the situation was outstanding. On the basis of this analysis, we would like to propose a brief interruption in our business relationship. We were thinking in terms of a twenty or thirty year pause!'

The two were delighted to have come up with this concept, especially the way they had formulated it. Never before had they looked forward so eagerly to an unpleasant call on a customer. The big moment finally arrived. They hardly recognised the person with

Don't aggravate yourself prophylactically!

- Don't aggravate yourself prematurely
- You're awaiting something negative, but the exact opposite then happens
- You're expecting hindrance and resistance and get the green light and open arms

What a pity for all that wonderful aggravation beforehand!

whom they had been doing business. No sooner had the customer seen them than he launched into a huge, cordial reception, hugged them, kissed them on the cheeks and said: 'You know, it's really a pity that we haven't done more business together in the past. I've always been impressed by your quality, your low prices, your dependability. Let's turn today into the start of something really big. Let's get going!'

It was as if the two visitors had been struck by lightning. There they were, sitting with their fascinating scenarios and they couldn't use them. What should they do? They were professionals, so they were flexible. They shifted gear immediately. They forgot about their scenarios and acted in accordance with the motto: 'Good, we'll take the money and forget about the triumph!'

Never start an argument over unimportant things

Does it pay to argue about this issue? Never touch issues if they will bring you nothing but aggravation in return. Many issues are complete theatres of war! Never make complaints that produce nothing but aggravation.

This is the success story of a father who succeeded in freeing himself completely from one type of aggravation. He reports:

> For months now, I've had no aggravation with my 20- and 22-year-old sons. In the past, though, there used to be constant aggravation.
>
> I've always told my sons, 'Children, press your jeans before you wear them to the opera.'
>
> 'Children, you inherited such beautiful hair from your mother. You got such wonderful hair genes. Do something with it. Try going near a barber shop!'
>
> Nothing happened. Finally, I realised that my power was limited. I can't change the two. I can only change myself.
>
> So I changed my clothing. The way I dress now, the hobos call me 'brother'.
>
> The way I wear my hair, young men on the bus stand up and offer me a seat with the words: 'Mother, would you like my seat?'
>
> I wear an earring! Now, my sons are beginning to fear that they'll wind up without any inheritance: 'You can't go around this way, what's going to become of you? You're ruining our reputation!'
>
> For weeks now, the two have been setting a good example for me. I don't think they'll have much success with me, though. Their agitation and aggravation are too relaxing to me!

Never start an argument over unimportant things!

- Does it pay to argue about this issue?
- Never touch issues if they will bring you nothing but aggravation.

Many issues are complete theatres of war!

Don't ask aggravation-triggering questions if you are not going to receive a sensible answer anyway. Aggravation land mines are scattered everywhere. Once you've recognised them, there is certainly no need to try them out.

Be friendlier to those who deserve it

Somebody has aggravated you. Don't pass on the aggravation. Be especially friendly to the next person you meet. You might be familiar with the old saying: 'You can't make a gift of friendliness, because it's always returned to you!'

And the person at whom you smile after you have been aggravated will return your friendliness to you. It is amazing how quickly your aggravated frame of mind will disappear if, instead of passing on your aggravation, you radiate kindness and cordiality. So smile after you've been aggravated. A smile is just as intolerable to aggravation as the sight of a cross to Count Dracula.

Show more patience and understanding. Often enough, people who are burdens to you are themselves burdened. Often enough, people who aggravate you are themselves aggravated. The taxi driver you had to wait so long for and whose late arrival upset you so much may perhaps have had to battle through stop-and-go rush-hour traffic. Look at the other's situation too.

Be generous and friendly. That way, you'll prevent aggravation. Pettiness, on the contrary, will heap aggravation upon you.

Contact land mines, action land mines and issue land mines are everywhere. Why, to say it once again, do you have to step on them intentionally and carelessly?

When you smile, you can't get aggravated. It is a physical impossibility. Smiling, by the way, is extremely efficient. Smiling is the facial expression that requires the least effort. It takes sixty-five muscles to frown. You only need ten for a smile. So when you smile, you get the facial expression for one-sixth of the normal price. Why on earth would you want to pay more?

Don't hurt others maliciously

Don't constantly make negative remarks. Abstain from unnecessary attacks and disputes. Refrain from making any cynical or sarcastic

It takes

65

muscles

to frown

But only

10

to smile

Why over-exert yourself?

remarks. Cynicism is the banner of childishness. Sarcasm is the self-awarded applause of the owner of a misanthropical intellect.

In the future, fight decisively to suppress every negative remark if it is not going to change the situation anyway.

Accept situations and events that you are no longer able to change without constantly lamenting and complaining about them.

You have to be able to conduct the following conversation. Your colleague says: 'Why are you simply taking that, why doesn't it aggravate you?' You reply: 'Can I change it?' Then comes the answer: 'But you could at least get aggravated about it!' And you respond: 'No, I don't care to!'

Don't repeatedly complain about people and events if you have long since resolved to bring about a real change at some specific time in the future.

Don't speak ill of those who are not present

Praise those who are not present. It will make them cheerful and relaxed. It is an outstanding method of aggravation prophylaxis. When you speak nicely about others, they hear about it. They know themselves quite well, feel that it is virtually impossible that you could have kind words to say about them, and nevertheless are happy about it.

Praise more, criticise less

Every word of praise that you voice lowers your blood pressure, every criticism that you make increases your blood pressure.

Don't discuss negative topics during meals

Negative topics are those that have 'gone sour'. But topics that have gone sour will sour your meal. Coming to the table with topics that have gone sour is even worse than coming with unwashed hands.

No negative topics late in the day

Don't start thrashing out negative topics late in the afternoon, in the evening or just before going to bed: 'I'd like to discuss a very unpleasant topic with you. Please don't go to sleep yet, I still have to tell you something that will give you bad dreams!'

No negative topics:

- **During meals**
- **Late in the afternoon**
- **Before going to sleep**
- **On Friday afternoons**
- **Just before going on holiday**

No negative topics that you soon forget but that others remember their whole life long!

Don't discuss any negative topics on Friday afternoon. Don't discuss anything negative before sending someone off on holiday. The rule, 'We have to give them something to think about while they're on holiday!' is not exactly the nicest way to treat other people.

Purge 'yes, but' from your vocabulary

'Yes, but' is a challenge. You stop others in their tracks and block the way. They rush at you, but you stand your ground. You collide, and they either steamroller you or go to their knees.

'Yes, but' is the exact opposite of the principle that is employed in all successful types of martial arts. These are based upon using your opponent's force not to block but to steer that opponent in a direction that is favourable for you.

You don't have to use *your* force to stop the other person. On the contrary, what you have to do is to utilise *the other person's* force.

This is the principle that manifests itself in the formulation: 'Yes, and . . .' Here, the other person's force is steered in a direction that is favourable for you. 'Yes, and . . .' is the judo method of argumentation.

Enough said about arguments and disputes. In principle, the rule is just as suitable for positive conversations.

With 'yes, and . . .', you understandingly pass from your partner's statement to a formulation that expresses sympathy and empathy.

'Yes, but' is not the key to the door behind which sympathy and empathy are waiting. Show your sympathy. Let others vent their aggravation. Don't block their desire to get it off their chest.

Don't immediately strike back with a careless remark. Look, listen and give others a chance to express what they want to say.

Perhaps you think what your marriage partner is talking about has no importance whatever. You can't understand why that subject is so irritating and stressful.

Listen. Perhaps you will learn how deeply your partner is affected and why this is so. Don't say that it's all unimportant and second-rate from your standpoint. From the other's standpoint, it is important and first-rate.

Show understanding and sympathy. Listen attentively and sympathetically. When you act this way, you will mitigate the confrontation. There will be fewer battles, more peace and less aggravation.

Voluntarily waive rights that are unimportant

Don't attempt to assert each and every claim you may have. Decline to assert rights if your success will hurt you more than it will benefit you. Never assert rights without considering the consequences: 'Here lies Mr Smith. He never yielded his right of way!'

No one else will ever again be able to steal the right of way that you have generously and courteously yielded. Gifts bring pleasure not only to the recipient, they give even more pleasure to the giver. Generosity makes you cheerful. A dogmatic attitude brings you nothing but aggravation.

Having doggedly to refuse the same thing over and over again is also aggravating. You are constantly being badgered to give your consent to something. Someone who repeatedly tries to do this to you usually has the better nerves.

These strong nerves are especially pronounced in the case of five-year-olds. Five-year-olds who want to have their own way possess imagination, argumentational skills and the siege potential that would have made the Turks in front of the gates to Vienna green with envy. When it comes to these things, five-year-olds possess the kind of potency that most sales managers would like their sales forces to have.

It is difficult to resist these kinds of strong personalities. They have the convincing power of a steamroller.

Perhaps all that refusing or holding out is doing is repeatedly and constantly to put you in a bad frame of mind. Perhaps you are only refusing because these kinds of requests are normally refused. Perhaps your consent would cost you nothing at all, but would offer you significant advantages.

Should this not be the case, you still have another option available to you: agree enthusiastically in principle, but insist upon something in return as a condition for your agreement.

Here is an example: a father is speaking with the headteacher of his son's school at the urging of his son. He asks the headteacher to transfer his son to a class that is being taught by a teacher that his son had last year and likes very much.

The headteacher's reply is: 'Of course, with pleasure, no problem at all. Your son should have the teacher he likes.

'I have only one request, though. Please find a pupil who would like to leave the teacher your son wants and would switch classes with him!'

Everyone immediately realises that it will be impossible to find this pupil. The discussion is over. The good-byes are cordial. The enthusiastic willingness to help was there. Unfortunately, though, conditions did not allow this good will to bear fruit.

Less resistance, less aggravation

You know one of the main causes of aggravation. It results when you want to get ahead and are being held back.

You have an idea, the others are opposed to it. You have a plan, the others block it. You want a decision, the others don't.

Each of us has to deal with professional anchors. These are people who are especially active when the need arises to prevent major activity.

You yourself come with a truckload of ideas and projects. The others let the air out of your tyres and then retire from the scene again.

The correct tactical approach therefore has to be different. You mustn't come with your truck, but with their truck. You mustn't start with your issues, but with their issues.

You always have to start with your business associates. You have to begin with their words, their ideas, what they value and what they consider to be important.

You have to link what your colleagues have with what you want. You take off in their plane, land in your plane, and wind up with the result you wanted.

Anchors who aggravate you are concentrating exclusively on the negative upper corner of your proposal.

It is in this corner that they set up camp. You can explain that this corner is not negative, but they will prove to you that the opposite is true. You can argue back and forth together and never get anywhere.

It is better to forget about your opening statements and start by asking questions. Ask whether this upper negative element, if it is really negative at all, will have any effect, whether it is relevant.

Ask the anchors whether they see anything good in the overall proposal. They will be taken aback and say: 'Of course, we merely wanted to point out that it also involves a negative factor!'

Thank them enthusiastically for calling your attention to this. Then move on to a discussion of the positive aspects.

Less resistance = less aggravation

Use others' force to move in your direction!

Don't start with yourself, start with them

- **Their words**
- **Their success**
- **Their ideas**

Link what they have with what you want

Avoid risk contacts

A murderer is someone who steals all of the remaining time that is available to someone else. Partial murderers are constantly on the prowl in every organisation. Not just the time murderers, but also the mood murderers.

Mood murder is a felony. Many professional criminals are active in this field. You have to protect yourself against them.

When you've had an extended conversation with some people, it takes two days for you to recover from the depressed state of mind that they have put you in.

Perhaps you cannot avoid contact with these mood killers. However, you should restrict your contact with them as much as possible. When dealing with this class of criminals, the contact-strategy watchword is: 'minimum contact'!

Stipulate the people with whom you do not wish to have any further contact at all. Draw up a 'blacklist' of topics that you will never again discuss with certain people. These kinds of people also include the idea thieves, for example.

There are some people with whom you should only speak on the telephone, but never meet with in person. You should only deal in writing with others, and then use only an absolute minimum of words.

Overstress nurtures aggravation

When you are overstressed, you become more irritable. When you become more irritable, you are quicker to get aggravated. A programme to combat your overstress is thus also a programme to combat aggravation.

Include time reserves in your planning. Everyone attempts to guard against risks by forming financial reserves. Everyone knows that they need financial reserves. However, this necessity is not seen as clearly when it comes to time, even though time reserves are especially important in maintaining quality of life. Without time reserves, your situation is just as hopeless as it would be without financial reserves. However, only a few of us are accustomed to including time reserves in our planning.

One example illustrates this quite well. Many people determine the time that will be required for a conference. But they do not

Risk contacts!

Less contact with typical aggravation provokers!

No contact at all with whom?

Only deal with some people on the telephone, instead of meeting with them personally!

Only deal with other people in writing, instead of on the telephone!

include in the plan enough time to prepare for the conference and usually any time at all for the follow-up work, for tracking what has been set in motion and for handling the promises that were made at the conference.

Don't overdo it with your obligations. Don't haphazardly agree to obligations. In particular, identify the magnitude of the obligation that you'll be faced with in connection with every new project. Calculate the obligation in terms of its time requirement.

Don't accept any deadline obligations that will put you under too much pressure and make you dependent upon others. If necessary, forgo financial gain if doing so will give you time and freedom of action.

The greater your ties to others, the greater your potential for aggravation. Consequently, keep these obligations and ties to a minimum. You don't have to be involved in everything. You don't have to grasp at every contact that comes along.

Don't mix everywhere. Don't force yourself upon others. Back off. Make contact only when it is really necessary. Avoid any obligation that is not absolutely necessary. An obligation that you accept is nothing else than giving someone else a claim on you. In other words, you are giving power over you to others.

Every time you start something, think about how it will end. As soon as you get yourself into something, think about how you can get out of it again easily. Keep your routes of retreat open. Napolean would have disappeared from the world political scene much earlier if he had not always observed this principle of strategy.

Don't terrorise yourself!

Don't be your own terrorist. Don't terrorise yourself with senseless, self-invented and self-dictated goals.

Think about what you will be able to do. Don't plan to do more today than you can really accomplish. Don't vainly attempt to do this, and that, and this, and then something else today.

Usually, it merely looks as if you're starting a lot of things but hardly ever able to complete anything.

Promise less

Many people promise too much. While they are making the promise, they are concentrating totally on making a wonderful impression at this very moment. With their promise, they want to arouse the favour of their business associate and prevent disfavour from arising.

They scatter promises from their cornucopia like spring scatters new flowers over meadows. While they are making their promises, it is virtually impossible for them to assess whether they will later actually be able to keep these promises.

Many people can keep only a fraction of the promises they make. They lack the time. Only a few hours after making a promise, they come out of their trance and begin to aggravate themselves about their own carelessness and lack of caution: 'What have I got myself into again this time? Was that really necessary?'

Every promise that you make to someone else is a time debt that you are assuming. Debts are aggravating. That's why, when making promises, you should attempt to pay in cash. This means that, if at all possible, you should be able to keep a promise that you make during a meeting before the meeting is over. The better you are equipped for the meeting, with information and documentation, for example, the easier this will be.

If you have what you promise with you, you will not be faced with a subsequent burden. So the right equipment is also a stress- and aggravation-prevention tool. What you do immediately is finished and done with. What you promise is a new load on your shoulders.

Get used to doing more immediately, instead of promising to handle it later. The earlier you handle something, the easier it will be for you. Every day you do not handle it will make it more difficult for you to keep a promise. And when a certain number of days have passed, it will be virtually impossible.

'Anyone who tries to hurry me is my enemy'

Someone who tries to hurry you is exercising power over you and aggravating you by doing so. If you promise something to someone precipitately, you are letting this other person get too close to you. There is no longer any time *cordon sanitaire* around you. Your liberty and freedom of action are restricted.

Never promise anything precipitately. Preserve your leeway. Don't carelessly put yourself under pressure. Don't say: 'I'll call you at nine o'clock.' It's better to say: 'I'll call you between nine and ten o'clock!'

If possible, don't say: 'I'll call you in the morning.' It's better to say:

'sometime during the course of the day'. Unless it is absolutely necessary, don't promise anything for 'Wednesday'. You'll feel under much less pressure later if you've said: 'on Wednesday or Thursday at the latest'.

The rider or the horse?

Aggravation is also a response to the pressure under which you have been placed. Avoid obligations that you enter into yourself but that enable others to put you under pressure. Don't create your own slave driver. Sooner or later, you have to decide what you want to be: 'The rider or the horse?'

Organise yourself better

Take sufficient time to complete important tasks. This will prevent aggravation later. Formulate instructions carefully. Concentrate when you read texts and read them exactly. Make notes during telephone calls.

Prepare thoroughly for meetings. All this serves to prevent aggravation.

Organise everything in such a way that you can work comfortably. You have to be able to work without distraction, without unrest, without chaos, and above all without your momentum being constantly retarded.

You should organise everything in such a way that your progress will not be impeded. You know that aggravation is produced when you want to get ahead and are prevented from doing so.

When you have organised things in a way that will allow you to progress smoothly and in a specific rhythm, you will be preventing aggravation.

Create a positive environment

Get aggravation-triggering reminiscences out of your sight. Free your walls, shelves and desk of objects that remind you of negative events or negative necessities. Surround yourself with objects that will immediately spark positive thoughts when you cast your gaze upon them.

Keep up your momentum – don't get out of the swing of things!

Organise everything in such a way that you can work *without being held back*:
- Without distraction
- Without unrest
- Without chaos

Organise everything in such a way that your progress will not be impeded. *Aggravation occurs when you are impeded.*

Organising things in a way that allows you to progress smoothly prevents aggravation.

Aggravation-triggering, irritating objects

Get them out of your sight!

- **No constant reminders of unsatisfied obligations**
- **No monuments in commemoration of lost battles**

Positive mental hygiene
Surround yourself with objects that
spark a positive frame of mind!

Objects can terrorise

No object is entitled to stay with you

just because

- **it's expensive**
- **it's valuable**
- **it's a gift**

Entitlement to a residence permit:

1. **Functional value**
2. **Aesthetic value**
3. **Symbolic value**

Launch a ballast-liberation programme

The more objects that exist around you, the more sources of stress and aggravation there are. Objects can terrorise you. The negative object that is not present cannot cause you any aggravation.

Many objects have long since ceased to have any function: they serve no purpose; they offer no benefit; they are unnecessary. They merely demand space and care, and in return they send you negative messages.

Create more order

Order provides you with inner tranquillity. It is the enemy of irritability. Order has an aesthetic component. Assign a place to each object. Return each object to its place again. You need enhanced clarity and should mark everything better. You should be able to reach out immediately and find what you are looking for.

Supplies

In the future, don't allow yourself to be aggravated any more because something is missing or has run out. Apply the techniques of purchasing and warehousing from your work life to your private life as well. Install an early-warning system that will show you what has to be procured. In the future, buy in larger quantity so that you will have a reserve supply.

Free yourself of thoughts that burden you

File your thoughts in an orderly manner. Don't constantly drag your thoughts around with you in your mind. Make notes of your thoughts. You should always have a pocket dictating machine within easy reach. That way, it takes only a few words to free your mind, and you'll never lose an important thought.

Don't aggravate yourself about what you can't avoid

Don't aggravate yourself about things that others force you to do. Decide whether you want to allow yourself to be coerced, or whether you have to. If you can't or don't want to refuse to do what others are

Create more order!

Order offers you inner tranquillity

Order is the enemy of irritability

- **A place for everything**
- **Everything in its place**
- **Everything *returned* to its place**
- **More clarity**
- **Everything labelled better**
- **Everything able to be found immediately by everyone**

How many minutes do you lose each day because you have to search for things?

asking of you, or if you *can't yet* refuse to do these things, the situation is clear. You have no other alternative.

Don't spend a single second aggravating yourself about the consequences. Even though you can't avoid doing something, you don't necessarily have to do it with a frown.

Don't overindulge others

Aggravation is the price that you will have to pay because you have overindulged others for much too long.

Carrying welfare to an extreme is a very special type of duress. A total welfare state is a slave state. It is not without reason that the term 'welfare terror' has been coined.

Carrying welfare to an extreme is not love and humanitarianism, it is the use of force that culminates in the other person being declared incompetent. This use of force is sooner or later avenged by the victim who is being cared for. At some point or another, the slave revolts. Excessive welfare later always turns against the benefactor who has been providing the care for too long.

Someone who has been indulged for too long becomes discontented and increasingly begins to make aggravation-triggering demands. If you have assumed full responsibility for another person for too long, that person will ultimately hold you responsible even for the weather.

Indulge others less. They will then make fewer demands on you.

Don't let yourself be turned into a slave

Refuse to go along with unreasonable demands: you can't satisfy every demand; you can't do what everyone wants; you can't please everyone; and you can't be a friend to everyone.

Determine which demands you feel are justified and which are not. Stipulate what you view as being unreasonable and have no intention of tolerating. Allow yourself to be neither pressured nor exploited.

Put up with less

Don't put up with annoyances for long. Don't wait until your nerves are already frayed before finally taking action. With more courage in your convictions, you'll have less aggravation. You'll have to be frank with some people. They don't understand any other language.

Don't put up with a lack of manners. Don't be especially solicitous towards those who are offensive. Don't chase after them and plead with them just to smooth things out. Give these people the cold shoulder.

In dealing with them, you have to be willing to sacrifice something; then you will almost never need to sacrifice anything. Impertinence is often the brother of cowardliness.

The sacrifice you might have to make is usually 'convenience'. It is possible that many of us put up with annoyances merely because resistance or the possible consequences of resistance could involve a loss of convenience.

The fear of suffering a loss of convenience is, of course, especially pronounced among those who are already suffering from a permanent lack of time and energy.

Don't allow yourself to be ignited by the surly, impudent behaviour of others. For example, an out-of-town couple arrives in a big city by train. They carry their luggage to the taxi line and ask the driver to take them to their hotel. The driver snarls: 'You could really walk the few hundred feet to the hotel!' They politely apologise. They didn't know, they say, how far the hotel was from the train station. The driver takes them there. They give him a £5 or, say, ($10.00) tip, in addition to the fare on the meter. He doesn't thank them, but merely drives off in a huff, grumbling and muttering to himself.

This happened in the morning. Until late in the afternoon, the couple is incapable of talking about anything else. The cab driver is 'constantly grumbling next to them'!

It is fascinating how totally insignificant events are able to sour our moods for so long. This is why you need desensitisation and a routine response to these kinds of occurrences. The cab driver has lots of cousins everywhere.

Don't attempt to buy the favour of these kinds of people by being calm and patronising towards them.

If you realise that you've come across this type of person turn the tables on them. Give them a few choice phrases that will stoke up their blood pressure so high that they will be able to drive even without the aid of petrol. Slip them a 10 pence (or, say, 10 cent) tip

Aggravation = anger

over your inability to defend yourself

against attacks from the

Grey Zone

- **Lack of manners**
- **Impertinence**
- **Ill will**
- **Deceit**

Weapons against 'grey-zone criminality'

are weapons against aggravation

Don't stand for as much

Don't wait until your nerves are shot
before reacting

More courage in your convictions =
less anger

Don't be especially solicitous towards
people who are especially brazen

Be willing to sacrifice something – then
you won't have to sacrifice anything
Impertinence is usually the twin of
cowardliness

Don't put up with everything – stand for everything

Try reacting with a different style

Not:

- Agitated
- Grumbling
- Complaining

Instead:

- Cool
- Calm
- With questions
- Without insistence

and tell them to treat themselves to something special that they've been after for ages.

Tackle negative things quickly

Don't let negative things simmer too long. After giving considered thought to the matter, handle unpleasant things as quickly as possible. You know that the longer you postpone an unpleasant task, the harder it will be to come to grips with it. The weight of an unpleasant, unfinished task increases from day to day.

Don't shy away too long from making sacrifices that have to be made. Sooner or later, you are going to have to resolve the problem anyway. The sooner you do it, the less it will ultimately cost you.

Legal assistance

Secure legal assistance early on. Get your legal adviser involved beforehand, during the prevention phase.

Every successful performer has a manager, who handles the aggravating tasks for the performer. There is a division of labour. The manager is a problem-solving specialist, and is responsible for handling the aggravation. The performer, on the other hand, can devote his or her full attention to work and conserve inner tranquillity and presence for that work.

You can also delegate someone else to handle your aggravation. You don't have to do everything yourself here. There are professionals who can help you in these matters.

Make complaints the right way

Don't try to make complaints only in person or on the telephone. Make them in writing. Develop a special style for your complaint-making attitude. It pays, because time and time again it will be necessary for you to make complaints.

The right to make a complaint not only affords you the opportunity to call other people's attention to their mistakes, inabilities or perhaps improprieties.

What is more important, the reason for making the complaint also offers you a chance to improve relations with other people and to eliminate the causes of these types of complaints in the future. So

The weight *of an unfinished task* increases from day to day

Aggravation

↓

The right to make complaints

↓

The opportunity to call someone else's attention to:

- Their mistakes
- Their inability
- Their stupidity
- Their impropriety

Aggravation – the chance to make complaints the right way and:

- Make friends
- Develop special relationships
- Eliminate mistakes in the future
- Improve your own frame of mind now

take a positive approach in making complaints. You can get upset about the matter; but you can also use humour and clear up the matter with ease.

The waiter makes a mistake and short-changes you £5 (or, say, $10.00). You can now indignantly point out the error. But you could also say: 'I'd like another £5 (or whatever) from you, please, but only if you can really spare it!'

Keep your lips sealed

The words you don't utter are the words you won't have to eat. What you don't say can never cause you any aggravaton. Stipulate which topics and which types of information you want to keep to yourself at all times.

The less you tell others, the less they can use it to your disadvantage.

How often have many people said: 'It only happened because I couldn't keep my mouth shut!'

Improve your personal communication skills

Communication always concerns the recipient. Communication is the process of ensuring that the information really arrives so that it will be easier for you to get ahead. This applies to both partners, the person giving the information and the person receiving it.

Communication ensures that the interacting partners will be able to act quickly, easily and correctly. Aggravation is the consequence of misunderstandings. Misunderstandings are often the result of communication that is 'only' verbal. So do more written communication. It is more professional.

The guileless are less susceptible to aggravation

The guileless possess the talent of misunderstanding. They do not feel that they are the intended or affected parties. Their attitude is one of sweet innocence: 'It couldn't have happened that way. They couldn't have meant that!'

The opposite of the guileless are the 'supersensitive': 'The director said "Good morning!" to me today. All day long I've been trying to figure out what that could mean.'

The benevolent support of others

Gain the benevolent support of others. Motivate others to this end. Be quicker and more intensive in thanking them for their support. You will receive the help for which you thanked them again in the future.

Be generous. Gratuities number among the most profitable investments you can make. When you give a tip, you make someone cheerful, attentive, willing, active and caring. By giving a generous tip, you can accomplish in seconds what would take hours for a top cosmetologist to achieve.

Pettiness makes others surly and obstinate. It is fertiliser for saboteurs. All that pettiness brings is aggravation.

Organising assistance

Where can you get assistance? As a prophylactic measure, stipulate where and how you can obtain assistance for many tasks in the event of an emergency.

Put a label indicating the customer-service telephone number on every piece of equipment. Maintain cordial relations with your suppliers and their customer-service organisations. Learn the names of the people who work there and personalise your relations with them.

Make it easy for others to satisfy properly their obligations to you

Provide information in writing. Indicate exactly where you want to meet. Send a map. Stipulate what to do should you miss each other. Make it easy for them to contact someone else, just in case.

Give them several telephone numbers. Incorporate redundancy in everything you do, just to be sure. Provide a fall-back plan.

Don't keep others waiting. Someone who has to wait gets aggravated and angry. Someone who has to wait too long loses essential elements of their good upbringing.

Ease the worries of others

Free others of their insecurity. Ease their worries. Offer other security and inner tranquillity. Wipe away their doubts, questions and fears early on.

Offer preventative answers to questions that others might later have. You know from your own experience which questions can arise. Call attention to these questions. Provide clarity and unambiguity as early as possible.

Eliminate the possibility of misunderstandings

Provide complete information. Don't put anyone in the intolerable situation of having to come begging for additional information.

When the possibility of insecurity, misunderstandings and mistakes has been eliminated, you will have less aggravation.

Anti-aggravation programme for your partners

What causes aggravation to the members of your family time and time again? Find out. What aggravates your customers time and time again? Ask several of your best, most important customers. Customers who don't get aggravated can't pass on any aggravation to you.

Ask your staff what makes their work more difficult and what aggravates them time and time again. Staff who make progress without any major obstacles will not pass on any aggravation to you.

'Zero defect organisation'

Strive for a 'zero defect organisation'. This applies both at home and at work. Motivate everyone you deal with to achieve this objective.

Make sure that everyone is alert and careful. Just because something has always gone well in the past does not necessarily mean it will in the future. Don't allow the self-confidence and cheerful carelessness of the unsuspecting to talk you out of taking preventative measures that you deem necessary on the basis of your experience and your intuition.

Opt for better timing

Select more suitable times for doing what you have to do. Pay more attention to when you should do things.

Most people are more difficult to reach on the telephone after 9.30 a.m. You'll need twice as long to reach a destination during rush hour.

Correct timing will help you avoid obstacles and thus avoid aggravation.

Why do it at all?

Don't be in a hurry to go marching off. The first question before you do anything should be: 'Why should I do this at all?'

Is this action necessary at all? Plan more; prepare yourself better. You will then need less time to do the work. The more care and foresight you use, the less rushed you will later be.

Is what you want to go out and pick up really ready yet? Call first; then drive off.

Reconfirm appointments by phone, just to be sure. In so many instances, five minutes more preparation will save you twenty-five minutes when you actually do the work.

Struggling for what is senseless

Don't attempt doggedly to achieve something that is senseless, just because you are facing difficulties along the way to your goal.

'Why don't I give Mr Jones a call? There's no real reason to do so, but why not?'

'Why is his phone busy? Why is his phone still busy? I've been trying to call him for fifteen minutes now, and his line is always busy. It's infuriating. Why doesn't he ever hang up?'

Your secretary asks: 'Whom are you trying to reach?'

Answer: 'Mr Jones!' 'Do you have to speak with him?'

Answer: 'No, of course not. But his line is always busy!'

Incremental costs

Pay the incremental costs. You are about to make a major purchase. You are going to have to pay a considerable amount of money for it. You are also going to have to pay for all the extras.

Somewhere along the line, many decide: 'Enough is enough! I'm not going to invest a penny more.'

The optional equipment you refuse to buy might account for only 1 per cent of the total cost. But you think enough is enough.

Unfortunately, there is a law that applies here: '99 per cent of the financial outlay provides you with only 80 per cent or less of the

Aggravation about obstacles

**Energy and drive wasted in the struggle
for senseless goals**

**The more difficult it is for you to achieve
a senseless goal, the more doggedly you
will struggle for it**

**Many life-long relationships have been
established this way**

Stop!

desired satisfaction!' The rear-window defroster you didn't buy is a prime example of this in the winter-time.

With 1 per cent more financial outlay, though, you can obtain 100 per cent satisfaction. The incremental costs are what determine the level of satisfaction. The greatest changes occur in the borderline area. This is a law of strategy.

So in the future, pay the unpleasant additional 1–5 per cent. Often enough it will bring you 20 per cent more satisfaction. In other words: 'The low incremental costs are offset by enormous incremental benefits!'

20 per cent cause 80 per cent of the aggravation

Twenty per cent of the people, the tasks, the activities, the products, the equipment cause 80 per cent of the aggravation. This 20 per cent has a disproportionately negative effect.

Take a strategic approach in tackling the causes of aggravation that have a disproportionate effect. Eliminate sources of aggravation that you cannot change.

If a field of activity accounts for 10 per cent of your total success, but for 40 per cent of your total aggravation, you should ask yourself whether you might not be better off without this field of activity.

'Who is really dissatisfied?'

Only a few of those who are satisfied with you actually thank you. Many act in accordance with the following motto: 'Why should I be grateful, everything is okay!'

The situation is entirely different in the case of those who are dissatisfied. They are no silent majority; they are a screeching minority. A large percentage of them are very liberal with their criticism.

Ninety-nine per cent of your colleagues are satisfied with what you have to offer; 1 per cent of your colleagues might perhaps be dissatisfied. Virtually all of this group will be there with their negative comments. You hear virtually nothing from the satisfied ones. So it's easy for you to misjudge your performance. The chief executive officer of one of Europe's most successful fast-food chains, a pioneer in the field of fast-food franchising, seldom receives a letter of recognition. It is the negative letters that predominate. Which makes it quite difficult to judge how many millions of people view his life's work with admiration and amazement. He hears about the aggravation-triggering negative comments daily; but rarely does he hear about the enormous volume of admiration that people have for him.

Screening off irritations

Protect yourself against environmental irritations. Protect yourself against noise. Don't allow others to fill your mind with noise.

Pay any price to protect yourself against noise. Use soundproofed ceilings, soundproofed windows and soundproofed doors. The less unrest there is about you, the less you will be distracted. You can then concentrate on what is important to you and get ahead faster.

Many people are aggravation addicts

It would seem that many people need aggravation. For them, that shot of adrenaline is what a shot of liquor is to an alcoholic. Every source of aggravation exerts a magnetic attraction on them. They appear on the scene whenever even the most remote possibility of aggravation exists.

They always want to know for sure whether there will be aggravation or not. They are usually lucky: their expectations materialise.

These aggravation addicts feel that they are affected by everything. They are always the target and are always involved.

Success aggravation

Aggravation is the price and the result of a growing volume of work, a lack of time or a lack of success; or it can be the result of too much success that comes too quickly.

The greater your success, and thus your reputation, the greater the circle of people who want something from you. The greater this circle becomes, the more sources of aggravation are produced.

The progress you have made so quickly and successfully is always a composite of departments, divisions, territories and products.

Not all of the elements in this composite have progressed and grown at the same speed.

You are far ahead with many of these elements; others are lagging far behind. This lack of symmetry in the composite, this disharmony, causes you aggravation. Your dream would be for all of the elements in the composite to reach the same high level at the same pace of high-quality growth.

Seen by everyone

Those who are at the head of organisations are seen by everyone. They are visible to all and a target for many. They have more players and more opponents.

These people's success irritates others and arouses envy. Envy gets many people moving who are otherwise almost impossible to budge. Their envy and their jealousy make them active. This, too, is one of the prices you have to pay for success.

Your aggravation and the aggravation of others

Compare your aggravation with that of others. Think about the abuse to which politicians are subjected. What would your frame of mind be if you, your intelligence, your appearance, your integrity, your vocabulary and your manner of speaking were constantly being raked over the coals this way?

Think about the threat that is inherent in certain professions. If an architect loses a client, she could very well lose 30 per cent of her income. Her security foundation is thin. If a doctor with a successful practice loses a patient, he probably won't even notice it, as he is dealing with a greater number of clients. His security foundation is thicker.

Negative things – positive things?

Make a comparison between the positive events and the negative ones. Don't just concentrate on what annoys and aggravates you. Don't just look at the negative exceptions to the positive rule.

Determine the factors that are presently positive for you. What is especially positive for you right now at work and at home? Keep them in mind. Learn to value and enjoy them.

Focus on positive things. Ask yourself how you can make these positive things even better. Learn to utilise better the aggressive power of positive things and of things that are going especially well.

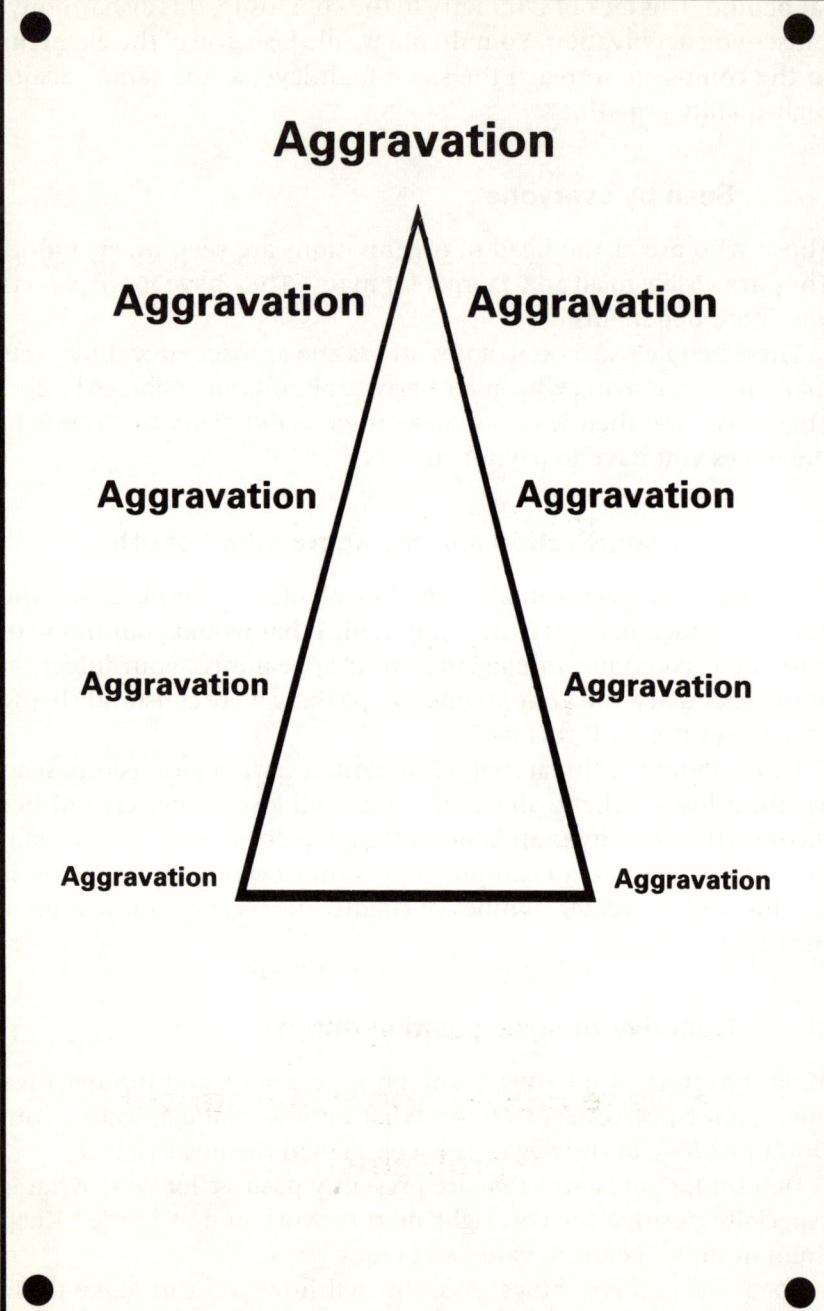

Success aggravation

Result of marching ahead too quickly

Price of leadership

High winds at the summit

- Visible to all
- Target for many
- More players
- More opponents
- More tasks
- More responsibility
- Less time
- More money (more investment
  problems)

Too generous?

In some exceptional cases, it can pay for you to be too generous. In these situations, you will ask yourself: 'Why should I at all; I'd be crazy; what a sorry state of affairs that would be; they'll think I've gone off my rocker if I concede to this demand!'

It may seem so at the moment; but life experience teaches that months or years later there will be a positive pay-back. It will far exceed what you once apparently so generously conceded.

Through your generosity you will be relieving someone else of an obligation. You will be setting someone free, even though there was no need for you to do so. In the eyes of the other person, you are suddenly a liberator. There are many people who will never forget that.

Don't aggravate yourself about having given more than you were obliged to. Instead, view what you have done as being a masterpiece of strategy.

Recognise that there is a type of behaviour that is guaranteed to lead to a catastrophe. This type of behaviour is resolutely and mercilessly exploiting every advantage and entitlement you have.

Don't aggravate yourself about the competition

Competition is necessary. It is a prerequisite for our freedom. Competition keeps you on your toes, it keeps you alert and flexible. And competition will be increasing at a pace that will not allow you to keep up with your aggravation.

Don't develop a negative attitude towards your competitors. It won't change anything. Get to know your competitors better. Be cordial and generous towards them.

Competitors are not merely opponents; they also have the power to repay you for your kindness and tolerance. Today's competitor might very well be tomorrow's colleague. Cordial behaviour towards competitors will put you at ease and give you a feeling of peace of mind.

Don't aggravate yourself about nerds

Nerds want to live too. Nature gave them the genes of a demolition contractor. So don't aggravate yourself about amateurish, nerdish and unprofessional behaviour. Set a positive stage that will make it impossible for nerds to pursue their work of destruction.

Be more creative in finding ways of turning everyone that you constantly have to deal with into people who act professionally and carefully. You will need more time and concentration to issue instructions that are more understandable, because it is better communication that protects the nerds against themselves and the idiotic things they do.

You will need to take more time for planning, preparation, training, post-mortems and for tracking and reviewing activities.

Don't make long explanations

From a given size onwards, an explanation becomes increasingly confusing and harder to understand. Say what you want briefly and concisely. Don't add any fillers. Do't start off with long introductions. Say: 'yes' or 'no'. Don't say' 'Let me put it this way', 'I would say', 'I tend to think', 'If push comes to shove I might not be completely indisposed to it'!

Keep up your blood-sugar level

Don't wait too long before eating. Don't starve yourself. Hungry people are irritable; people with a full stomach are content.

Responding to aggravation

Develop a response routine. When an aggravating event occurs, a phase of shock sets in. It paralyses reason and triggers reactions that are rash, wrong and senseless. Be aware of this phase of shock. Go into your calm mode and take a break.

Don't get yourself worked up. Don't immediately swing into action. First determine what has 'really' happened. Perhaps you merely misunderstood what was said.

The aggravation avalanche

Often enough, what triggers the aggravation is merely a snowflake. Your emotional reaction turns it into a snowball. It begins rolling downhill and sets off an avalanche. It takes hours until the victims of this avalanche have crawled out again.

Then they spot the chief snowman who had acted so carelessly.

Here he comes, with his bad conscience, to help in the rescue effort. His frown has turned into an embarrassed smile.

Your most recent aggravation

Think back and recall your most recent aggravation. The interactions that aggravation involves are impressive. All that is necessary is for the right players to meet up. Within minutes, they are capable of creating aggravation, of turning the place into a zoo. How much time have you lost recently as a result of the wrong reaction to aggravation? How much money have you senselessly wasted? What negative obligations have you committed yourself to? Which associations have you damaged? How much have you done to your reputation?

Verbalise your aggravation

Pick up your dictating machine. Dictate a checklist containing all of the points that will help you prevent this kind of aggravation in the future. Get your aggravation off your chest to free yourself of it and, at the same time, to prevent this variety of aggravation from occurring in the future.

Don't try to handle the aggravation immediately. First transfer it from your mind to a list. Dictate or write the aggravation out of your mind. Dictating the aggravation is like using a fire extinguisher.

Delegate someone else to handle the aggravation

You yourself are too irritated at the moment. Don't deal with the aggravation yourself. Someone else who is more objective will have an easier job here.

You don't have to get back for everything

Someone has aggravated you. What's the point of returning the aggravation? You don't have to start a ping-pong match. Simply let the other person's aggravating ball roll off into the bushes. Don't even turn around to see where it went. Let the matter simply die its own death.

Petty reaction

Stupefy the other person with the exact opposite of your previous reaction. What would be a petty reaction to this occurrence? Which discussions, which actions?

Study your typical behaviour patterns when this type of aggravation occurs. This is the behaviour pattern that others are familiar with. Whom do you contact? What do you say? What do you do? How do you act an hour later, a day later? This time, act completely differently!

The aggravation findings

Every instance of aggravation deserves a diagnosis. Sometimes only seconds are needed for it. By doing it, you will save yourself from producing an avalanche. If you don't set off an aggravation avalanche, you won't have to blame yourself for it later.

In the case of aggravation, too, the therapy has to be preceded by a diagnosis. Frequently, the aggravation diagnosis is the therapy. Often enough, a diagnosis will show you that no action is necessary.

Don't dramatise things

When an aggravating event occurs, keep your strong imagination from going into action: 'That does it, I'm going to leave my job as a teacher and go into politics!'

Frequently, the event will not have any impact at all. Usually, the impact will be less than what you fear. You'll be able to handle what results.

Quantifying aggravation

Quantify the importance of the cause of your aggravation:

1. What will be its financial impact?
2. What will be its time impact?
3. What will be its effect on my security?
4. What will be its effect on my reputation?

Destructive imagination

Don't work yourself up emotionally. Don't be steamrollered by your

The significance of this aggravation –

quantified in figures:

1. Financial impact?
2. Time impact?
3. Effect on your security?
4. Effect on your reputation?

• No effect at all?

• Negative effects only – or positive ones too?

Which ones?

80% imagination

20% facts

- **Don't let your imagination run wild**
- **Don't panic**
- **Don't get hysterical**

Take a more realistic view of the magnitude of the possible consequences!!!

Remember:

'Where there's a will there's a way!'

imagination. Much of what you are viewing in the darkest colours are not facts but pure imagination.

Eighty per cent is imagination and not more than 20 per cent fact. Take a more realistic view of the magnitude of the possible consequences of this aggravating event. Take a more relaxed view of the possible consequences.

Can you change it?

Can you undo what has happened? Is there anything about this matter that you can still change? If not, why should you get excited about it? Will you still be aggravated about it tomorrow? Will you still know the day after tomorrow what you were so aggravated about two days earlier?

What will happen if you lose control of yourself now? What will you lose in terms of time, energy and your frame of mind? Do you want to sacrifice today to your emotions? Do you want to wash away today in a bath of acid?

Do you absolutely have to get upset about it just now? Do you have to deal with this aggravation immediately; isn't there anything else that is more important?

Write down your aggravation; then it can't be lost and you can still decide later how you want to act.

Remember that aggravating yourself will not make you any stronger. Aggravating yourself will make you neither stronger nor more intelligent.

Don't ruin what you had planned for the day

Don't let your day be ruined by the aggravation. Don't start wandering around to tell everyone who has the misfortune to be reached by you about the unfortunate occurrence. Don't start calling everyone whose line is not busy.

Imagine that you can't reach anyone. Wherever you call, all that you hear is an answering machine. Wouldn't it seem funny to start telling fifteen answering machines about the idiotic thing that just happened to you? 'Hello answering machine: you won't believe what I've just heard . . .'

Full of compassion, the answering machine then concludes the conversation: 'Your aggravation has been registered. Thank you for your call. Please hang up now!'

Reverse the effect of aggravation

Ask yourself how you can neutralise or reverse the negative effect of your aggravation. You have two questions available to you for this purpose:

1.   What shall I do about this aggravation?
2.   How can I utilise this aggravating event for my own purposes?

You can view the aggravation as an opportunity. The grand art of handling aggravation is to employ the aggravation as the point of departure for a successful campaign.

Aggravation puts you in contact with whoever was responsible for the aggravation. You can call them to task, attack them and fight them because of the aggravation.

Or you can also simply guilelessly assume that the aggravation was serving as a type of marriage broker to get you together with the person who caused it.

What are the positive consequences that you can draw from this confrontation which has been brought about by the aggravation? You might be able to turn the confrontation into cooperation. What counts is perhaps not the aggravation but the contact that it has produced.

Expert 'complaint handlers' know what is meant here. They utilise a complaint as an opportunity and turn the customer who is making the complaint into a business friend.

The quantum leap into the future

Stop viewing the past and the present as quickly as possible. Don't just ask how all this could have happened and whether it had to be. Make a quantum leap into the future.

Switch to the prevention mode and ask yourself: 'What do I have to do to eliminate this kind of aggravation in the future?'

Put the results of your thinking into checklist form. Stipulate it in an operating procedure. Set the above-mentioned 'positive stage', i.e. do a better job of organising.

A new attitude

How do you want to make it easier for you to cope with this kind of aggravation in the future? How do you want to change your attitude

Anti-aggravation questions

Can I undo what happened?

How can I reduce its negative impact?

How can my positive action
- neutralise
- reverse

its negative impact?

How do I have to react to the event to
turn it into a success?

Quantum leap

What has to happen to avoid this kind of aggravation in the future?

- Verbalise it
- Get it off your chest
- Out of your mind and onto paper

- List of aggravation
- Operating procedure
- Checklist

towards this kind of aggravation? Which basic decision do you have to make now? How will you act in the future if these kinds of events should occur again?

The end of the tunnel

When have you reached the end of the tunnel with respect to this aggravation issue? When will this kind of aggravation no longer occur? When will the conditions have changed? What have you initiated to this end? Which strategic decisions have you already made?

Four kinds of weapons for combating aggravation

You have at your disposal four kinds of weapons with which you can combat aggravation:

1.   *Prevention* = eliminating risk factors.
2.   *A new attitude* = a different way of looking at certain types of aggravation.
3.   *A new response routine* = a different way of acting when aggravation occurs.
4.   *The strategic solution* = rigorously bidding farewell to sources of aggravation.

Anger at being helpless

Aggravation is often nothing other than being angry about your own present helplessness. Aggravation is produced when you do not have the time to parry an attack appropriately.

Reference has already been made to the importance of time reserves. Let us emphasise it once again. You should never fully plan your time. You need time reserves. Only then will you be able to respond quickly and aggressively to annoyances and attacks.

What do you never want to get aggravated about again?

What do you never want to get upset about again, never discuss again and never conduct unpleasant discussions about again?

What are you no longer willing to accept? What do you want to

Anti-aggravation

- **Prevention**

Eliminate risk factors

- **New attitude**

Look at certain types of aggravation differently

- **New response routine**

Act differently when aggravation occurs

- **Strategic solution**

Bid farewell to sources of aggravation

Basic decision!!!

What do you never want to get aggravated about again?

1. _____
   _____
   _____

2. _____
   _____
   _____

3. _____
   _____
   _____

4. _____
   _____
   _____

5. _____
   _____
   _____

Bid farewell forever!!!

**Parting with an old companion named
'aggravation'**

**'You've accompanied me long enough
now.
You're beginning to get on my nerves.'**

**Good-bye.
Find someone else!**

eliminate as quickly as possible? Write down the answers to these questions. Make the decisions.

Today is the great hail and farewell party for any number of aggravating circumstances. After having lived intimately with them for decades, you are now preparing to blast them into outer space.

Attacking aggravation physically

Work off your aggravation physically. Do some gymnastics. Take a brisk walk. Climb a few flights of stairs. Exhale the aggravation; breathe it away.

Aggravation, the grand source of ideas

View aggravation as being a prime source of ideas. It can supply you with innumerable ideas for improvements.

You can determine the direction in which your aggravation will work. It will either work against you or for you. Either it attacks you or you attack it. You are either its victim or it is your tool.

Aggravation is a true service organisation. Aggravation provides you with 'full service'. It supplies you with the raw materials for a different attitude, with better principles, a more practical outlook, measures, methods and tools.

Aggravation supplies you with approaches for improved communication and cooperation.

Aggravation supplies you with more than just contentual information. It also supplies you with the drive to put an end to what has thus far been robbing you of your frame of mind.

View your present aggravation as a mechanism for initiating improvements. Aggravation presents itself to you as dual system. It is a system that provides you with ideas and with the drive to implement these ideas.

It is up to you to decide which effect your aggravation is going to have. Everything depends upon your reaction. Aggravation either saps energy from you or supplies it to you. In the future, view it only in positive terms, as fuel for the rocket of change. *Aggravation begins with an 'A', as in 'alter'.*

Anti-aggravation system

=

'Creative system'

Aggravation = a super source of ideas

Causes of aggravation?

1. Lack of professionalism

2. Strategic mistakes

3. Lack of planning

4. Organisational deficiencies

5. Lack of prevention

6. Clutter

7. Obstacles

8. Communication errors

Aggravation shows you almost everything!

People who are quick-witted have less aggravation

Most of us are unbelievably quick-witted

The aggravating part of it is:
We're usually too late with our quick wits

Aggravation and worry

Use the same principle you employ for other tasks

A set weekly appointment

**Wednesdays
from 11.30 a.m.
to 12.00 noon**

Your new reaction routine

Before:

Aggravation = destroying the present

It attacks you

Now:

Aggravation = fuel for the rocket of change

You attack it

Aggravation begins with an 'A', as in alter

CHAPTER 4

Avoiding anxiety and improving quality of life

Courage is a crucial virtue. More than almost any other factor it determines your quality of life. One of the greatest combinations for success consists of courage, professionalism and charm.

Improvements in your quality of life are directly related to reductions in your timidity. Courage compounds your quality of life. Courage makes you different from the others. It is something out of the ordinary.

Fear spoils everything

Timidity has a negative effect. Usually, it doesn't even relate to major threats but to possible occurrences of ridiculously minute magnitude and impact.

It is fear that puts you in the position you want to avoid

Study your biography. Which decisions have you made out of panic and fear? What consequences did this have for your life and your family?

From which key negative decisions that you made out of fear do you still suffer? What are the catastrophic situations in which your fear of a possible situation has put you?

Many people have ended up in a present catastrophe out of a fear of the future. Fear sets the switches the wrong way.

Courageous, but not foolhardy

When many people hear the word 'courage', they automatically think of the offsetting gift of the gods to those who got the short end of the stick when intelligence was passed out. When judging the term 'courage', many assume that it can be possessed only by those who lack the ability to assess the situation.

Of course, this type of fearless personality does exist. It is a characteristic trait of vital and enthusiastic dilettantes who are willing to leap into every catastrophe with the greatest of ease.

These are the kinds of fearless individuals who are especially courageous when others have to bear the consequences.

So what we are not talking about is the courage of a driver who is hurtling down the road and does not know that the bridge around the next bend has collapsed.

Nor are we talking about the naive optimism that is the exact opposite of professionalism. The optimism of the naive is: 'Everything will work out somehow!' The optimism of the professional is: 'I'll do everything possible to make sure it's not a flop!'

Of course, courage must be paired with care and prudence. The unsuspecting individual in the midst of chaos is by no means the fearless individual. Courage is not a lack of caution. Of course, it involves thinking in terms of prevention. Thinking in terms of prevention is *the* prerequisite for courage. A fair amount of caution is there too; however, everything is perceived in an aggressive and resolute manner. Courage leads you to an offensive form of prevention and defence. That is the mental point of departure.

The reward for courage

Courage increases your freedom of action – it makes you independent. You do not automatically wrap yourself up with people and tasks.

Through courage, you protect yourself against chaos. Courage is your suit of armour and your shield. Courage leads you to take the offensive. Every human being needs to take the offensive. Someone who is on the offensive is in an entirely different frame of mind from a soldier in a retreating army.

Courage is the key to many doors. In fact, it is the main key.

Courage and the courage of one's convictions impress others and keep them at bay. Fear, on the contrary, turns every situation to your disadvantage.

Courage is the basis for peace of mind

You'll be transformed from the anvil to the hammer. You'll shape your life yourself. You'll increase your joy in living and preserve your cheerfulness.

Fear robs you of your frame of mind and of the strength to act.

Only if you are courageous will you possess the prerequisite for getting ahead quickly and decisively. You will not be paralysed. You will tackle difficult problems. You will not waver. You will not constantly be changing your goals.

You will pursue the opportunities that present themselves with vigour. You will not give yourself the order to stand still. Nothing will be too difficult for you if you are fearless.

Courage prevents resignation from setting in. You'll become stronger in power struggles. Faced with the alternatives of 'battle or subjugation', you will choose to fight.

Courage enables you to say 'no'. It prevents resignation from setting in. It puts you in a position to show no weaknesses.

You will no longer be dominated by excitement, panic and hysteria. There will be no petty back and forth.

When you are fearful, your inner unrest prevents you from completing a task. You flee from one half-finished task to another.

You feel that you are under constant pressure to take preventative measures. Frequently, these are measures that are unnecessary from an objective standpoint. Only fear drives you to do these things. Fear causes you to lose an incredible amount of time. You are constantly forced to cover yourself preventatively or reactively.

You're looking for crutches

You are constantly taking on new tasks because you fear that you will one day stand there without any support. When you are fearful, you seek the security of a crutch. But in reality the crutch does not support you. Instead, it keeps you down or with your back to the wall.

Over the course of time, the crutch, which is really a burden, becomes a vital necessity for you. If you no longer have this crutch, you topple or tremble in freedom.

Freedom of action without a restrictive support has become intolerable for you. You are incapable of being alone for long, free periods of time without the supportive and securing effect of a constant burden.

Fear and talkativeness are twins

Fear destroys your self-discipline. Many conversations owe their existence to fear. However, you can only preserve your freedom if you are closed-lipped.

Being talkative out of fear makes you dependent and vulnerable: on the one hand, you are unable to handle many important issues and to articulate yourself precisely; on the other hand, you are overcome by a pathological urge to talk and communicate. Fear produces a tidal wave of words.

Courage opens the door to charm

Courage is the basis for amicability. It would be entirely one-sided to view courage merely as a means of overcoming resistance and prevailing in your goals.

Courage is also needed for an embrace. It is not merely battle gear. It is also a prerequisite for demonstrating affection.

Affection, too, is an act of force; kindness, too, requires peace of mind. Since you have no fear, you have no fear of saying or writing something nice to someone. You praise unabashedly. You offer the gift of recognition, without asking how it might be received.

You can live your life yourself

You can shape your life yourself. You can change what you do not like. You can reject what you do not want. You can establish contacts and end contacts. You can win partners and leave partners.

You act faster and more resolutely. You don't waste time thinking about how to plan your leap across the chasm. You simply leap. You defend your time. You fight doggedly for appointments that fit in with your schedule. You don't allow yourself to be rushed. You become calm, more relaxed and more courteous.

Madariaga describes the image of a person who walks tall. For him, there are tree people and herd people. You can choose to be a member of a herd. Then you are protected by other bodies. But you are no longer free and unencumbered. Only courage can free you of life in the herd.

With courage, you make others more successful. This applies with respect to your marriage partner, your children and your staff. You make life easier for others. You take away fear and replace it with cheerfulness. As a fearless person, you are a benefit to humanity, especially to that part of humanity that is closest to you.

What you need is a courage programme

A courage programme includes philosophical rules, principles of strategy and methods.

You need to make basic decisions about dealing with others and your own personal style. You need a 'rhythm' of courage.

Analyse the causes of your inner unrest, which can range all the way to fear. Fear is often the lack of concrete numbers. Should you view a possible development with fear, attempt as soon as possible to quantify the magnitude of the threat in the form of numbers. The less blurry you view the situation, the less fear will remain.

View obstacles as being a normal part of life

Don't let yourself be paralysed and emotionalised by these obstacles. Stop contemplating; start acting. Move ahead.

Tackle a difficult problem with the enthusiasm of someone who knows that the advantages gained from solving the problem will be enormous. And one of the greatest advantages will be the positive turn in your frame of mind.

Develop a peace-of-mind routine

Hectic activity is ridiculous. Force yourself to be calm. Move from fear to cheerful peace of mind. An attitude that can best be described as relaxed, cheerful and cordial belongs in your 'style programme'.

Don't respond to threats with panic

Don't immediately over-react. Wait before making concessions. Stand your ground. Don't let others push you away.

Be militant. Overcome obstacles cold-bloodedly. Pursue your

objectives with resolve and with a sense of priorities. Do what you fear immediately. Pick up the receiver and make the telephone call.

Be less dependent upon stimuli

Desensitise yourself. Become less dependent upon stimuli. You will have to become less susceptible to the influence of threats, impending dangers and the entreaties of the panic makers.

Don't allow yourself to be terrorised and swept up into a negative frame of mind by your imagination. Calculate the financial and security impact of a given threat. Ask yourself how the new situation would look. Then think about the options that are available to you and which preventative measures must be taken now.

Speak a courageous language

Throw the fearful words out of your vocabulary. Use positive words that signify courage.

Purge all of the negative stories from your repertoire.

Become courageous by changing your manner of speaking. Speak slowly and calmly, distinctly and loud enough. Look the person you are talking with in the eye.

Purge fillers and waffle from your conversations. Do not be afraid to pause when speaking.

Don't make the sad sighs of self-consciousness: 'Er, er, er!'

Courage and aesthetics

Use the means of aesthetics to boost your spirits. When it comes to courage, a good frame of mind is half the battle. Make your environment positive and optimistic. Choose better lighting. Put beauty and brightness into your environment.

Recognise your security

Determine what it is that you mean by security. Base your thinking upon a specific expectation of what life should hold for you. Compare what you need with what you have and with what you could get along with.

Courage is having a knowledge of resources, possessing alternatives and the resolve to get along with the bare minimum if need be.

Planning

Don't attempt to strive for courage by means of a 'one-year view and plan'. Don't always base your thinking on only a one-year time frame.

Budget for a longer time frame. And do the same with your time budget.

Analyse possible threats

Work out contingency plans. Ensure positive results by spending more time on the following:

Preparation.
Prevention.
Back-up measures.
Cultivating relationships.

Don't let yourself be intimidated

Don't let yourself be treated like a weakling. Don't chase after others. Don't court the friendship of brutal people.

Don't constantly be making explanations. Don't always be apologising. Don't be reproachful. Don't conduct agitated arguments.

Don't allow obstacles to discourage you. Don't be depressed because things are not progressing or are not progressing fast enough.

Fear neither what others might say nor what others might do. Don't allow yourself to be so impressed by what others say and do.

Advocate your standpoint with courage and charm towards people you like; do it with courage, severity and courtesy towards the others.

Don't attempt to satisfy everyone at any price. You can't do it. If you try, you are doomed to failure.

There is an extreme form of taking pains towards others. It deserves the name 'unworthy zeal'. This type of behaviour will be rewarded with neither security nor recognition.

Many people cannot tolerate friendliness. This word is foreign to their vocabulary. They automatically confuse friendliness with weakness. So determine the people with whom friendliness and kind efforts will get you nothing except the exact opposite of what you had intended.

You can't change everyone

Sooner or later, you make the last attempt. Then, the only alternative is to change yourself. In the case of certain circumstances, situations and people, the only recourse that is left to you is resignation: 'Here I stand, it can't be helped!'

When that happens, it is quite possible that the other person will recognise the resignation with which you view the situation. But that doesn't suit the other person either, who then changes only because you no longer thought it would be possible to change. Then, you will have achieved what you wanted from the very beginning. The strategic formula is called: 'Only when you have decided to do without something will it be given to you!'

Optimistic associates

Learn more about contact strategy. The quality of your life is determined by your selection of associates. With whom do you want to be together? With whom do you not want to be together? What opportunities are available to you here? Whom do you want to keep as far away from you as you can?

Be together more with optimistic and courageous people. Have no inhibitions about getting to know people who possess these qualities.

Courageous people don't need to terrorise others. They are content with themselves and do not have to grab the territories of others. They let others live in freedom and enjoy the existence of other free people.

Only weaklings can't stand free people. They hate them. One of these weaklings actually said the following words: 'That person is too self-assured for me!'

That says it all. The defamation and hatred from another person just because there is someone who is stronger.

Keep people like this away from you. Don't waste your time on the poison mushrooms.

The associates you need are not the creatures of the night, but people with a sunny disposition. There are enough of them around. You'll find them where courage reigns supreme.

Look forward

Exercise care, but not cautiously. Overcaution retards your ability to perceive enormous opportunities.

Do you have an offensive or defensive mentality?

The defensive mentality sees a difficulty in every opportunity; the offensive mentality sees an opportunity in every difficulty. The defensive mentality asks: 'Where won't it work?'

The offensive mentality asks: 'Where will it work?'

For the defensive mentality, a solution is only viable if it will work everywhere and all the time. The offensive mentality finds it outstanding if it will work in even 30 per cent of all cases and simply goes on to seek further solutions. The defensive mentality demands the philosopher's stone; the offensive mentality starts a stone collection.

People with a defensive mentality dig themselves into a trench of their own making. They allow others to determine where the battle will be fought. They respond to what others force upon them. Those with an offensive mentality launch an attack and are the ones who choose where the battle will be fought. They act.

The defensive mentality bemoans the development. The offensive mentality takes note of it, influences it and decisively utilises the opportunities it offers.

The defensive mentality answers: 'Yes, but . . .'

The offensive mentality answers: 'Yes – and that's why . . .'

People with a defensive mentality do not change their routine until they are forced into doing so and have no other alternative. Those with an offensive mentality are constantly doing away with routine that has become meaningless and go about developing a better routine.

The defensive mentality concentrates on circumstances, methods, tools and means; the offensive mentality concentrates on people.

Those with a defensive mentality view cultivating the favour of associates as chasing after them, a waste of time and a loss of prestige. Those with an offensive mentality enjoy people and like to cultivate their favour. They do so with cheerful peace of mind and self-assurance. The response to their efforts makes them even more optimistic.

The defensive mentality complains; the offensive mentality grasps

Fear is the mother of failure

What could he . . .

What could she . . .

think

say

do

Key tasks

- Take away fear and anxiety
- Be calming
- Impart confidence, a positive frame of mind
- Motivate
- Give strength

He who allows the
impossible
to cloud his view for the
possible
is a fool!!!

(Carl von Clausewitz)

the bull by the horns. The defensive mentality looks after sacred cows; the offensive mentality eats steaks.

The defensive mentality talks; the offensive mentality acts.

The defensive mentality asks: 'Why?'

The offensive mentality asks: 'Why not?'

The defensive mentality has objections, while the offensive mentality has ideas.

To those with a defensive mentality, everything is always totally different. In their case, everything is special. They have no use for methods from other sectors. Those with an offensive mentality, on the other hand, feel that many others must be facing the same situation. So perhaps they have solutions that can be of use.

The defensive mentality uses the vocabulary of defence: 'That's not allowed; that won't work; that won't work everywhere; that won't always work; that won't work for everyone!'

The offensive mentality needs only one sentence: 'Do you think you might have another good idea?'

People with a defensive mentality say: 'It's all theoretical!' Those with an offensive mentality say: 'Thank you very much!' The defensive mentality poisons every wellspring of ideas; the offensive mentality cares for them, cultivates them and keeps them flowing. The defensive mentality paralyses associates and destroys their self-confidence; the offensive mentality makes them active and capable.

The offensive mentality knows that new problems also bring with them the need for new solutions and has the motto 'No problems, no opportunities!'

An offensive attitude strengthens creativity. It overcomes fear and puts life into life. But when the corners of the mouth begin to droop, ideas leave the mind and the sun disappears behind the clouds.

A defensive attitude breeds ill humour; an offensive attitude spawns cheerfulness. Cheerfulness is contagious and gives courage – to you and to everyone you like.